SONYA FAURE

HIDEAWAYS

CABINS, HUTS, AND TREE HOUSE ESCAPES

Flammarion

*To my parents,
to Maud, Gaële, and Elsa,
to our hideaways at la butte de Candy
and in the garden of Montsoult,
and to Fabrice Barthélémy for his time.*

Contents

OVER THE THRESHOLD

And so I am cheered by the pictures I find in my reading. I go to live in the "literary prints" poets offer me. The more simple the engraved house the more it fires my imagination as an inhabitant. It does not remain a mere "representation." Its lines have force and, as a shelter, it is fortifying. It asks to be lived in simply with all the security that simplicity gives. The print house awakens a feeling for the hut in me and, through it, I re-experience the penetrating gaze of the little window.

The Poetics of Space, Gaston Bachelard

A few steps along a rickety jetty, a cycle ride along a blustery sea wall ... Hideaways merit a special effort. Beach huts vary enormously in style: dignified along the strand in the Stockholm archipelago, and humble on a spit of land jutting out from the Brittany coast near Dinard (preceding pages). The sheer tranquillity of a beach hut is a rare treat in the modern world, as in this hut made of planks in Cap Ferret, near Bordeaux (facing page).

Hideaways. The word evokes a world of whispered secrets, stolen kisses, and preciously guarded childhood treasures. It hardly seems a fitting title for a serious book. How about *Cabins* or *Cottages*, which sound more grown-up, more serious? But hideaways are more than just buildings. They can be a hut or a shed, a chalet or a tree house, built on piles on an African lake or on the roof of an apartment block in Paris, nestled in the sand-dunes of the Belgian coast, or high in the mountains. The one thing they all have in common is a rather poetic concept of what architecture is about. Their designers and owners see them first and foremost as a place to seek refuge from the strains and stresses of daily life, a kind of sanctuary from the pressures of modern society. Every hideaway has a story to tell—a thousand variations on the well-loved tale of Robinson Crusoe, who built the desert island hideaway many people dream of. The adventure begins with planning and building the hideaway, and continues for as long as it is visited and cherished, whatever it is used for—hunting, gardening, writing, or simply reading the afternoon away, curled up in a cozy armchair.

Hideaways have always been a feature of gardens and parks, not to mention playing a role in numerous folk tales, but interest has certainly grown in them over the last few years. In France, for instance, the Ministry of Education and the French Institute for Architecture made *hideaways* the theme for a project intended to get schoolchildren thinking about architecture. A number of specialist design agencies have been set up by men and women who fell under the spell of hideaways as children, and tour operators have begun to latch on to the trend, offering short breaks in yurts or in underwater cabins. Hideaways have also been the theme for several exhibitions and garden festivals. Town halls have begun renovating the sheds on their allotments as a way of inducing people to take pride in their local community. Hideaways even have a serious political dimension: the growing number of shacks built without permits and blocking public access to beaches has recently become something of a problem in the

south of France, as in Corsica and Copenhagen. As pressure on available housing resources grows, and prices for land spiral ever higher, the trend is towards do-it-yourself, smaller homes, more innovative design making the best use of space, and the use of more environmentally friendly building materials.

If hideaways are currently the height of fashion, considered by many as a potential solution to the housing crisis, it is because they represent a simpler, more intuitive approach to man's relationship with his environment. Hideaways represent values opposed to some of the least appealing aspects of modern society. They are small and intimate, unlike the chilly modernity of many loft developments. They are hidden in gardens and forests, well protected against the pollution of our cities. Their simple charm makes a mockery of our high-tech solutions. Hideaways invite you to switch off your pager, Palm Pilot, and mobile phone, and relax. Improvisation is the watchword of hideaways—a world away from our daily routine where every minute must be accounted for and there is no time to stand still and watch the world go by.

Some of the best things about hideaways are the fact that they are environmentally friendly, often built using recycled materials, close to nature, and reflecting the personality of their owner. Yet these features can survive only if hideaways remain beyond the reach of mass production. The danger of standardization, which would completely kill off their charm, is already emerging in the use of hideaways in advertisements for everything from olive oil to tropical-scented deodorants.

There is no easy, standard definition of what counts as a hideaway. Each hideaway is different, and while the structure may be planned, chance, and above all imagination, also have a hand. The finished hideaway is a happy-go-lucky combination of local traditions, architectural trends, and personal tastes. Often, the hideaway is not designed with a single purpose in mind. It is simply planned as a pleasant place to go and read, play, work, paint, or just sit and dream. The ethnologist Laurence Nicolas describes the hideaway's function as follows: "A vacant, uncertain, unfocused, or wild place located on the borders or margins. The hideaway's territory can in fact be defined as being 'beyond territory.' Where they are not simply banned, they are at best tolerated, or sometimes ignored or kept secret. Anywhere can be a hideaway, as long as it transgresses our ordinary categories of space." Hideaways like to keep their secrets. Each hideaway takes on the shape of its owner's deepest desires. By their very nature, hideaways are discreet. To define and study them, an oblique approach is called for.

Perched in the crown of a gigantic oak tree, some forty feet (twelve meters) above the ground, the tree house belonging to the photographer Yann Arthus-Bertrand stands high above les Mesnuls, near Paris. The designers of this luxurious nest admit to having suffered from vertigo so high up in the branches. Once inside, it is a charmingly cozy, warm nest, all in wood, worthy of Robinson Crusoe himself.

Everyone occasionally has the urge to get away from it all, make a break with routine and all the stresses of modern life, and spend even just a few hours in utter solitude. These barns, converted into mountain hideaways (facing page), are the perfect place to escape from it all. Dream the winter away in a hut set in endless fields of snow in Quebec (right), or imagine whiling away the days fishing and collecting shells on a beach that stretches as far as the eye can see. Following page: a few huts mark the beginning of the channel that runs along Tremblade beach—the longest in France.

The dictionary defines a hideaway as "a secluded spot." It is a small, often temporary structure, and can be as simple as a lean-to made of branches. There are plenty of synonyms for the word, most of which emphasize its protective function: cover, den, haven, hideout, refuge, retreat, sanctuary, shelter. A hideaway can be a lean-to, a shed, a cubbyhole, a chalet, a gazebo, a shack, a wigwam, a teepee, a yurt . . . the list goes on. The noun "hut" and the verb "to hide" share the same Indo-European root, *skeu-*, meaning to cover or conceal. Hideaways have always been associated with concealment—whether it be lovers meeting in secret to declare their flame, children hoarding their treasures, or authors seeking seclusion to finish their latest masterpiece.

Hideaways came into vogue in Europe in the eighteenth century, when philosophers of the Age of Enlightenment such as Jean-Jacques Rousseau were rethinking the nature of human society, private property, and the influence of architecture on human behavior. Hideaways are only necessary in societies which place a premium on individualism and privacy. But while the concept of the hideaway dates back to the beginnings of our modern society, they are, by their very nature, ephemeral. As time passes, the structures become ever more fragile. Often the work of groups in search of an alternative lifestyle, they usually do not outlast the community they were built for. In an increasingly homogenized world, hideaways, reflecting as they do a highly personal vision of what a building should be, go against the grain. The shacks in the village of Beauduc, in the Camargue region of southern France, have been a thorn in the side of the local authorities for years, as their inhabitants resist all attempts to "tidy up" the village, demanding the right to live as they choose. As the ethnologist Bernard Picon says, hideaways run counter to the idea of a disciplined, tidy world.

It is the last word in luxury to own a place specifically devoted to relaxation and inactivity. In the right place—on the Bassin d'Arcachon in France, on Martha's Vineyard or Cape Cod—a getaway cottage can be a source of social prestige, for which people are willing to pay the price. In the genteel seaside resort of Southwold in eastern England, a beach hut measuring eleven by twelve feet will set you back a cool £45,000 ($75,000). Once you have bought or planned your hideaway, you are free to do with it as you like—often, the usual building permits do not apply (although you should check with the local authorities first)—as free as Huckleberry Finn asleep in his barrel, or the nobleman in Italo Calvino's novel *The Baron in the Trees*.

The hideaway is characterized by these paradoxes and ambiguities. It is a threshold, a gateway, which allows a passage from the stresses of the modern world, where time is at a premium, to a more peaceful, tranquil place, where you can spend hours watching raindrops racing each other down the window-pane. Stepping back into the modern world, you feel relaxed, as if your batteries have been recharged.

CHILDHOOD HIDEAWAYS

"Yes," Tintin concluded, "that's right, we must find some corner, a hiding place or a hole to put all the stuff."

"What if we built a hideaway," La Crique suggested, "a super hideaway in an old quarry, properly sheltered and well hidden…."

"It would be jolly," said Tintin, "a real hideaway, with mattresses of dry leaves to rest on, a hearth for lighting fires, and where we can have parties when we have some money."

The War of the Buttons, Louis Pergaud

This little boy sitting in a willow hut in a Kent garden seems utterly absorbed in the book he is reading, lost in another world.

Say the word "hideaway," and the memories of childhood come rushing back. Rainy Sunday afternoons spent building a fortress of cushions on the living room floor. A magical summer spent playing pirates in the lofty branches of a tree turned by enchantment into a Spanish galleon. The reassuring smell of sawdust and motor oil in grandfather's shed as he turned a set of bowling pins on the lathe. Such hideaways are often the first notion children have of architecture, the place that protects them and helps build their identity, giving them the confidence to face the world beyond their home. The hideaway is symbolic of a desire to return to our innocent childhood selves. The story of Robinson Crusoe is the symbolic retelling of the childhood of humanity.

Learning through play

Never did the Celts facing down the thunder with bows and arrows, or the glorious journeymen of the century of cathedrals sculpting their dreams of stone, or the volunteers inspired to join the Great Revolution by the stirring words of Danton, or the leaders of the 1848 uprising planting the tree of liberty, undertake their task with such joyous ardor and frenetic enthusiasm as the forty-five soldiers of Lebrac, in an old quarry lost in the meadows and woods of Saute, when they set about building their shared house of hopes and dreams.

The War of the Buttons, Louis Pergaud

In Louis Pergaud's classic children's novel *The War of the Buttons*, written in 1912, a gang of children set about building a shed as a rite of passage on their way to manhood. There, they light fires—dangerous, fascinating, and utterly forbidden at home—and drink stolen bottles of beer. These scenes will ring a bell with many children who had the good fortune to grow up in the country, where there are still abandoned outbuildings and charcoal-burners' huts to explore when the lure of a hot, sunny afternoon entices them away from the classroom. But what about the children who live in towns and cities? There, the only lawns and trees are in parks, where they are ordered to keep off the grass. Their vision of nature is one of pruned trees, carefully weeded flowerbeds, and swept-up piles of leaves. What hideaways do these children have, apart from their bedrooms, fully equipped with video games and televisions?

Many urban children have never tried to make something on their own from scratch. They have no idea how to plan a design, or how to cut, fold, and stick things together. A growing awareness of this problem prompted the French Ministry of Education, in conjunction with the IFA (Institute Français d'Architecture), to launch a program in 2001 to encourage children to take notice of the built environment. The program, entitled "Build your own adventure," was welcomed by primary school teachers and architects, who worked with children to design and build a hideaway, either in the classroom or in the playground. The project was taken up eagerly by classes all over France, from Paris to the overseas territory of Réunion in the Indian Ocean. The children rediscovered the joys of designing and creating something from scratch, and even if the final result was rather chaotic, the lesson had been learned. Many of the designs were extremely imaginative, using recycled building materials donated by the local community, or plastic bottles in place of planks of wood, decorated with cut-out crepe-paper flowers. Many of the designs were inspired by fairy tales—the witch's gingerbread cottage in "Hansel and Gretel," "The Three Little Pigs". Some designs were based on picture-book illustrations of

Hideaways play an important role in childhood. They help children develop a sense of space, let them express their own personality, and give rein to their imagination. A temporary hideaway (facing page) designed by schoolchildren in the Paris region, provides a place for storing their most precious possessions: a handful of marbles or a collection of pretty shells. The brightly colored structure resembles a giant turtle, straight out of a fairy tale.

As part of a recent project designed to introduce children to architecture, groups of schoolchildren all over France designed their own ingenious, inventive huts and hideaways. Near Paris, a hut inspired by snail shells; in the central Puy de Dôme region, a play hut full of light and as airy as a butterfly's wing, made of recycled plastic bottles and CDs; the children of Réunion, in the Indian Ocean, decided to make a "wild hut" using a recycled washing machine, soda cans, plastic chairs, and old tires.

prehistoric families in their caves, while others were built using an old car, cardboard boxes, or plants, in the shape of a man or a snail shell. The children's designs were charming, spontaneous, adapted to their own scale. All in all, the project proved an excellent way to introduce children to architecture. They learned how to work together to overcome unforeseen problems in their designs, and gained valuable practical skills.

One particularly interesting project was organized by the architect Frédéric Nantois in a class of seven- and eight-year-olds in a Parisian primary school. He asked them to imagine an alternative ending for the story of the three little pigs. After much discussion, the children decided that the third little pig's house of bricks—the one the wolf cannot blow down—was too staid and unimaginative for their taste. They thought it was unfair that the houses of straw and sticks, that looked much more fun to live in, should be blown down by the wolf, and so they decided to invent a fourth little pig, living peacefully in a house that the wolf never managed to find. It is a charming story, with a serious point: the children came up with an original and inventive design for a house that could be dismantled in minutes, should the wolf happen to pass by. The fourth little pig's house was a dome with an ultra-light structure made of everyday materials—wood, Saran wrap, and a hose-pipe—with paper flowers scattered over it as camouflage.

To begin with, many of the children had a rather rigid view of what constituted a proper hideaway. It was not just a small house or even a spaceship. Nearly all of their early drawings were of a wooden structure, either at the foot of a tree or in its branches. Maybe this is an urban child's idealized dream of life in the country. Many of the children also said they had never played in a hideaway, apart from a lucky few who spent the weekends and vacations with their parents or grandparents in the country. However, when asked where they liked to go when they wanted to be alone, their imaginative use of space became apparent: they played under tables or under a sheet draped over two chairs, in a large cardboard box or under the stairs.

Wherever children live—in a tiny village or in a great capital—they turn to their hideaways for the same reasons: to have a secret place where they can see without being seen, a place to rest and be alone, and a place where they can be with their friends without adult supervision. They want to play hide and seek, soldiers, and mommies and daddies, come up with daring plans of attack on the kitchen pantry, or be alone with a favorite book. It is important for children to have access to a place they can call their own, where they can begin the important work of growing up and facing the world—a place with a door they can choose to open or keep shut. This is how children learn to respect the intimacy of others as well as themselves. Building a hideaway is a step on the road to building their own personality.

This hut, designed by children under the supervision of the architect Frédéric Nantois, belongs to the fourth little pig— the one the wolf never managed to find . . . It is well camouflaged, with a roof of rubber sheeting full of holes artfully disguised with crepe paper flowers.

A hideaway is a child's private space, an outpost from where he can spy on the adults around him, and where he can sit and reflect about what he has learned. Whatever form the hideaway takes, it plays a vital part of the child's learning process—helping him assuage his curiosity about the world around him—and is a shell he can hide in like a tortoise when he is tired or sad. Child psychologists point out that when they are aged six or so, children believe that their parents can read their minds and discover what they are thinking. A hideaway gives them the freedom to think whatever they please without worrying about what their parents will say, and to be angry at them if they feel the need. The psychoanalyst Didier Anzieu says that children shut themselves away in hideaways as if in a prison cell, to punish themselves for what they perceive to be bad thoughts.

The act of choosing a hideaway is symbolic of the child's desire to build up a distinct personality. In order to do this, he may borrow or even steal from his parents to create his own treasure trove. Ten-year-old Julie has fond memories of the hideaway on the edge of the forest where she spent her last vacation: "I go there with my sister when we're fed up with our parents. We play board games and eat sweets we've stolen from them. And when my big brothers tease us, we hide there until things blow over."

One particular feature is always prominent in children's drawings: the door, which symbolizes the threshold, the frontier between inside—where the child is the master—and outside, where he depends on his parents. Inside, it is up to the child to decide who can come in and what games are played. Inside, he can see without being seen, and learns how people behave when they are unaware that they are being watched. This is why children usually choose a hideaway close to their home, in the garden or the living room, like an isolated bubble in a world of adults. Like Italo Calvino's baron in the trees, they take a step back from the world, the better to observe it: "From the tree Cosimo looked at the world; everything seen from up there seemed different, which was fun in itself."

The threshold of the hideaway is a guarantee of privacy, symbolizing the child's right to shut the door, turn the key, and spend some time alone. Children have the right to keep secrets. One of the children interviewed for the "Build your own adventure" project talked about the hideaway he made for himself by draping a bed sheet over the dining room table. This obviously gave him a much stronger sense of his own private space than his own bedroom did. His parents and sister did not knock on the bedroom door before coming in, but had to wait to be invited before joining him under the table.

The image of the shelter as a protective cocoon was particularly strong in one primary school class in Paris, where several children were recent immigrants from Ecuador, Sri Lanka, and Morocco. The architect Alexis Meier decided to make the different origins of the children the theme for the class project, entitled "A hideaway without borders." The children designed a structure that had no walls, and yet which was felt to be protective. The immigrant children obviously had different cultural references, and rather than drawing a tree house as their French classmates did, they came up with three startlingly original

This charming little round hut is perfect for whispering secrets and stealing kisses. Children love the little nest designed by Cyril Delage and Virginie Écorce for the Jardins de la Brande in the Dordogne (southwest France). The hut is made of chestnut wood and clay adobe, and was built using the traditional techniques of the coopers who strengthened their barrels with bands made of chestnut branches.

This palatial tree house (facing page) in Cheshire in the northwest of England is home in turn to pirates and buccaneers, Robin Hood and his merry men, Tom Sawyer and his companions, or Rapunzel in her lonely tower. It was built by the Scottish company TreeHouse some twenty feet (six meters) above the ground in the branches of a group of 250-year-old trees. It consists of several platforms linked by a number of rope bridges. On a smaller scale is the thatched hut (right) designed by the landscape architect Bunny Guinness in her Cambridgeshire garden.

plans: a hut covered in scales, an apple topped with a chimney, and a tunnel with a bell tower. Taking these drawings as a starting point, Alexis Meier then drew up plans for a hideaway that was closed off with rows of waves rather than walls. The design had no rigid borders, and yet the children were able to hide inside.

Children create their own rules when they play in hideaways, adopting codes of conduct that either imitate the rules of the adult world or, on the contrary, delight in transgressing them. So while the children defiantly eat with their fingers or talk at the top of their voices, they also play at being grown-ups. Like in the Countess of Ségur's nineteenth-century tale *The Vacation*, the activities tend to be strongly divided along gender lines: boys tend to use strength and ingenious inventiveness to build their hideaway, while girls are more preoccupied with organizing the interior and playing at housekeeping. Seven-year-old Alice, for example, has set up her hideaway in a garden shed in a run-down area of Paris. She likes pretending to be a teacher and playing with her dolls. There are books, bits of fabric, and dolls' teacups scattered all over the floor. Her mother says, "Here she is allowed to shout, tell off her dolls, and spill water. She can even light candles if she wants."

Children have always been fascinated by the terrible beauty of fire. The hideaway, a place of transgression beyond the reach of parents, is where they come to experiment. Louis Pergaud's *The War of the Buttons* explains this dangerous fascination: "Their wish would come true: their personalities were born of this act, done by them and for them. They would have a house, a palace, a fortress, a temple, a pantheon, where they would be at home, and where their parents, the schoolmaster, and the vicar—the great opponents of their projects—would not set foot, where they would be left in peace to do all the things they were forbidden to do in church, in class, and at home: slouch, take off their shoes or their jacket, or go naked, light fires, cook potatoes, smoke viburnum cigarettes, and above all hide their buttons and their weapons." Far from being unruly and undisciplined, the micro-societies established in the hideouts of the two gangs in *The War of the Buttons* have their own strict rules and codes of conduct. They hide from the uninitiated, organize ceremonies, hang mistletoe over the door because "that's what the Ancient Gauls did," and hide their loot like "a sacred ciborium in a tabernacle." They smoke, drink, sing, and make merry.

Other children like to flirt with danger in other ways, daring each other to hide in dark woods or spend the night in a deserted, maybe haunted, house, far from their parents and the protective walls of their home. Many little boys have spent a memorable summer reliving the adventures of Mark Twain's immortal literary creations Tom Sawyer and Huckleberry Finn: "Shortly Tom came upon the juvenile pariah of the village, Huckleberry Finn, son of the town drunkard. Huckleberry was cordially hated and dreaded by all the mothers of the town, because he was idle and lawless and vulgar and bad—and because all their children admired him so, and delighted in his forbidden society, and wished they dared to

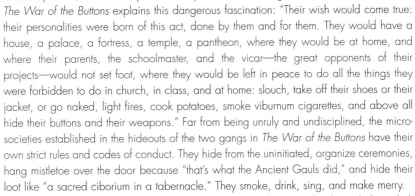

be like him. . . . Huckleberry came and went, at his own free will. He slept on doorsteps in fine weather and in empty hogsheads in wet" (*The Adventures of Tom Sawyer*). In the Missouri town of St. Petersburg, all the boys dream of tasting the freedom enjoyed by Huck Finn, without parents, brothers and sisters, or teachers to keep an eye on them. Huckleberry Finn lives free, in barrels, tents, hideaways, and wigwams. When Huck decides to lie low for a while on Jackson's Island, he hides in the woods: "I got my traps out of the canoe and made me a nice camp in the thick woods. I made a kind of tent out of my blankets to put my things under so the rain couldn't get at them. . . . the next day I went exploring around down through the island. I was boss of it; it all belonged to me, so to say, and I wanted to know all about it." Children like to play at scaring themselves and each other, and are endlessly fascinated by life in the heart of nature, where mysteries and danger lurk, where each crack of a branch could be a ghost, each rustle of leaves a wolf ready to pounce, and where they can hear their heart beating in the silence.

But hideaways are fragile. They represent a vital stage in a child's development, but it is inevitable that children grow out of them. Some children delight in knocking down the fortress they have spent so many hours patiently building. Others simply turn their back on them, and leave old toys lying forgotten in the dust and shadows. Occasionally, some children refuse to grow out of the hideaway where they have spent so many happy hours, using it as a protective shell against the world of adults. This is the case in Jean Cocteau's novel *The Holy Terrors*, where the children Paul and Elisabeth have constructed an elaborate private universe of codes and rituals that seals them off from the rest of the world. Their hideaway, in a magnificent town house, is their only world, a symbol of their exclusive, quasi-incestuous love for each other.

The next day Paul started building himself a private sort of hut, without a roof, with screens for walls, and settled in. Both in its outer eccentricity and its inner chaos, this curious enclosure seemed integrally designed to fit the unearthly aspect of the room. Paul brought along books, empty boxes, treasure and plaster to furnish it. His dirty linen began piling up.

The Holy Terrors, Jean Cocteau

Sleeping in a teepee or tree house is a real adventure. Who knows what monsters may come in the night? "For night had fallen and the water, now running more rapidly, was flowing with such power that I grew scared. In vain, snuggled in my shelter, I closed my eyes and tried to forget. I felt small, frail, reduced to this little bit of me trembling in an animal's lair." The Child and the River, *Henri Bosco.*

Standing lonely at
the crossroads, the hut
is a welcome sight for
heroes and travelers
lost in the dark woods.
Such huts are a
traditional feature
of folk tales, from
"Goldilocks and
the Three Bears" to
"Snow White" and the
terrible witch and her
gingerbread cottage in
"Hansel and Gretel."

Once upon a time

But now the poor child was all alone in the great forest, and so terrified that she looked at all the leaves on the trees, and did not know what to do....Then she saw a little cottage and went into it to rest herself. Everything in the cottage was small, but neater and cleaner than can be told.

Snow White and the Seven Dwarves

Hideaways play an important role in the folk tales of many cultures. However, descriptions of the huts themselves are rare. Only in a very few tales, such as "Hansel and Gretel" or "The Three Little Pigs," does the architecture of the hut play a role—in the first tale, the witch uses her gingerbread cottage to lure the children, and in the second, the wolf, having destroyed the house of straw and the house of sticks, is finally roasted coming down the chimney of the house of bricks. However, in the majority of folk tales, the hut is seen as a symbolic space for the hero to test his strength and wits against the wicked witch, rather than an actual building. Maybe the descriptions were deliberately left vague so that a child listening to the tales could imagine his own home, and himself as the hero.

Hideaways in folk tales are always set in clearings in dark forests. They represent a corner of the civilized world lost in wild natural surroundings. They are the shelter that magically comes into sight just as the hero was beginning to despair of finding a place for the night. The cottage is plain, modest, and simply decorated. In the tale "The Handless Maiden," one of the lesser-known stories by the Brothers Grimm, the maiden, who is so beautiful and good that the king chooses her for his wife, is tricked by the devil and must leave her husband's castle or else be executed. "She came into a great wild forest. There she fell on her knees and prayed to Heaven. The angel appeared and led her to a little house. There was a sign on it, with the words, *Here all dwell free. . . .* She stayed seven years in the little house, and was well cared for. And by Heaven's grace, her hands, which had been cut off, grew once more, because of her piety." Whatever form they take— dwarves, old women, shining angels—the magical figures who live in the cottages in the woods have a particular symbolic function. They reveal the true nature of the hero's mission. In another of the Grimm tales, "The Three Little Men in the Wood," a young girl is maltreated by her wicked stepmother. One day she finds "a small house out of which peeped three little dwarfs." To thank her for her gentleness and generosity, they offer her three gifts: "Said the first, 'My gift is, that she shall every day grow more beautiful.' The second said, 'My gift is, that gold pieces shall fall out of her mouth every time she speaks.' The third said, 'My gift is that a king shall come and take her to wife.'" When her half-sister finds out, she becomes mad with jealousy and seeks out the dwarves for herself. But she refuses to share her meal with them, and they curse her: she will become uglier every day, die a miserable death, and toads will pour from her mouth with every word.

The hut in the depths of the woods is sometimes a place where the heroes must defeat their opponents. Hansel and Gretel's new stepmother convinces their father to abandon them in the woods. There they wander, lonely, cold, terrified, and in danger of starving to death, until they spy a cottage. "When they came quite up to the little house they saw that it was built

An engraving by P. E. Tardieu based on an original by J. B. Oudry, illustrating Jean de La Fontaine's fable "The Wolf, the Nanny-Goat, and the Kid." Facing page: A hideaway made of bed sheets in Claude Ponti's book Okilélé.

of bread and covered with cakes, but that the windows were of clear sugar. 'We will set to work on that,' said Hansel, 'and have a good meal.' I will eat a bit of the roof, and you, Gretel, can eat some of the window, it will taste sweet.'" But the cottage belongs to a witch, who captures Hansel and fattens him up to eat until cunning Gretel helps him escape.

Hideaways in folk tales are passages to another world. They symbolize the transition from childhood to adulthood—a royal castle and a prince or princess to marry. To go from one to the other, the hero must pass through the liminal space of the cottage in the forest. In the tale "The Innocent Maiden," the young heroine seeks refuge in a hollow tree-trunk. The ethnologist Josiane Bru writes: "Like a protective roof, the hollow in the tree is an enchanted place. Its vaulted entrance, like a set of brackets, explicitly figures her temporary retreat from life. It is like a coffin, as she is believed to be dead."

The hut or cottage in the woods is reminiscent of the initiation rituals practiced by certain tribes, where the young people are sent into the forest to live in a hut where they will be initiated into adulthood. As Josiane Bru writes, "In the West, this transition takes place in a discreet manner, in folk tales or in games played in hideaways where children sketch out their own autonomous life and grow into adulthood." The hideaways in folk tales are places of passage, in time and space. The hero must pass through, but cannot stay for long. Only the dwarves, who will never grow old, can live forever in their cottage.

Dream hideaways

All really inhabited space bears the essence of the notion of home…we travel to the land of Motionless Childhood, motionless the way all immemorial things are. We live fixations, fixations of happiness. We comfort ourselves by reliving memories of protection.

The Poetics of Space, Gaston Bachelard

The word "hideaway" immediately triggers a wave of nostalgic memories. It is synonymous with the return to a golden, untroubled childhood. The child psychologist Franck Zigante believes that while children build their hideaways near their homes to be able to observe the adult world without being seen, adults prefer to daydream about being Robinson Crusoe, castaway on a desert island—of being totally alone. He says that while children's hideaways are a vital step in their psychological development, the type of hideaway generally preferred by adults reflects a need for reassurance and a sense of soothing security. Adults dream of regressing to childhood to escape from stressful or hostile situations. This can be a way of tuning out the constant stream of information that bombards us in the modern world. Hideaways represent a need to get in touch with the simpler things in life again. By seeking refuge in a hideaway, adults are subconsciously trying to reconnect with the early days of humanity once more, reliving the adventures of their earliest ancestors. This is why the legend of Robinson Crusoe has such resonance for us. In Defoe's immortal novel, the sailor is washed up on his island with nothing more than a pocket knife and a pipe. To begin with, he is totally lost. His first thought is to build a shelter: "I walk'd about the shore almost all day to find out a place to fix my habitation, greatly concern'd to secure my self from an attack in the night." As he builds his home, Robinson Crusoe recreates the society he left behind in Britain by giving the rooms appropriate names: "During all this time, I work'd to make this room or cave spacious enough to accommodate me as a Warehouse or Magazin, a Kitchen, a Dining-Room, and a Cellar." His home, however rough and ready, was his castle. There he felt safe—and powerful. "I was removed from all the wickedness of the world here. I had neither the lust of the flesh, the lust of the eye, or the pride of life. I had nothing to covet, for I had all that I was now capable of enjoying. I was lord of the whole manor; or, if I pleased, I might call myself king or emperor over the whole country which I had possession of." He leads a peaceful life, far from civilization, with no need for anything beyond what he is able to make or grow himself.

Huts and hideaways are emblematic of childhood innocence, a state of grace many adults dream of returning to. These hideaways have a powerful symbolic resonance, like basket maker Eric Renault's love nest whose walls seem to merge into the surrounding vegetation, at the Hauts-de-Seine garden Festival in France (left). Facing page: the charmingly bucolic hut at the Breuil gardening college in the Bois de Vincennes.

John Harris designs huts and hideaways in Scotland. He came up with this design for his Hideaway Hollow (facing page) because he wanted to enjoy the secluded atmosphere of a tree house although there were no trees in his garden. The "trunk," some twelve feet (four meters) tall, can be "planted" anywhere. It is a magical playground for children, who can explore the interior of the trunk, race up the spiral staircase, and play on the veranda. The Hideaway Hollow is on sale in the toy department of Harrods. This hideaway is a wildly imaginative design reminiscent of the Garden Sheds, a series of engravings by François Houtin (right).

How different from the stressful pace of modern life! Small wonder that so many people dream of escaping to a hideaway, to find themselves.

Robinson chooses to build his hut in an idyllic corner of his island. There is a deep-rooted need in each of us to experience nature on its own terms, as Robinson does. Hideaways are by their very nature fragile traces of the civilized world in the heart of nature, who delights in reminding us of her power and our frailty. We draw strength and sustenance from nature—and sometimes, nature overpowers us. The hideaway is then the last link with our everyday lives and our culture. In Michel Tournier's adaptation of the Robinson Crusoe legend, *Friday and Robinson: Life on Speranza Island*, Robinson first attempts to leave the island by boat, but fails, and gradually regresses, becoming almost an animal. He decides to take his life in hand, dares to face up to his surroundings, and sets out to build a real home so that he does not have to sleep in a cave or at the foot of a tree any more. He gradually claws back his lost dignity through hard work. The inhabitants of Jules Verne's Mysterious Island make their own nitroglycerin, glass, bricks, and a hydraulic elevator for their "shelter," Granite House. In these cases, the hideaways can be defined by the owners' desire to come to terms with their surroundings, rather than the style of building.

In his masterpiece *The Poetics of Space*, the philosopher Gaston Bachelard wrote of the symbolism of the hut and dreams of a primitive life, of the powerful sense of warmth and comfort we feel when we snuggle up in a hideaway. "For instance, in the house itself, in the family sitting room, a dreamer of refuges dreams of a hut, of a nest, or of nooks and corners in which he would like to hide away, like an animal in its hole [...] But in most hut dreams we hope to live elsewhere, far from the over-crowded house, far from the city cares. We flee in thought in search of a real refuge." Like dogs, hideaways come to resemble their owners, the people who imprint them with their personality and tastes, who entrust them with their secrets. Their very humbleness is reassuring, because we know that there is no room for arrogance. They are places of trust. Gaston Bachelard sums up the irresistible magic of the hideaway: "Primal images, simple engravings are but so many invitations to start imagining again. They give us back areas of being, houses in which the human being's certainty of being is concentrated, and we have the impression that, by living in such images as these, in images that are as stabilizing as these are, we could start a new life, a life that would be our own, that would belong to us in our very depths."

HIDEAWAY HOMES

*It is in an old buccaneer's cabin that I opt to take shelter. When the
wind blows in off the sea, fog holds down upon the boulders of the
coast, and little by little the beach disappears in a cottony cloud.
Then I see nothing but the bones of whales, I hear nothing more
than the groaning wind. The great jaws jut up everywhere in the
sand like arcs, and the backbones seem like columns of stone broken
in some cataclysm.*

Pawana, Jean-Marie Le Clézio, tr. Christophe Brunski

*Alain Laurens has
made his home in the
branches of an Aleppo
pine in the Lubéron
(southern France). As
the former chairman of
an advertising agency,
he likes to joke that he
has swapped one jungle
for another. He even
has his meals sent up
to him in a basket
on the end of a rope!*

Staying in a hideaway is always a chance to make a break with daily routine. People often dream of getting away from it all, living alone, tuning out the white noise of daily life and getting in touch with their inner selves. Once peacefully settled in a hideaway, time can be lavished on reading, writing, painting, or just relaxing. Hideaways are enchanted spaces beyond the reach of time. Going to a hideaway, even just at the bottom of the garden, is taking a step back from life to taste the joys of solitude, the better to enjoy the return to family life. It takes a conscious effort to learn to enjoy wasting time—although, of course, time spent relaxing is never wasted. A hideaway is an act of resistance against the pressures of modern life. It is a journey back to our true selves.

A voyage around my room

It is a cottage of quite a peculiar kind, for it is only ten feet square and less than seven feet high. All the joints are hinged with metal so that if the situation no longer pleases me I can easily take it down and transport it elsewhere.

The Ten Foot Square Hut, Kamo No Chomei, tr. A.L. Sadleir

No more watches to wind or timetables to stick to. . . . Nothing but a door to open and a step to sweep clean, brushing away the soft heaps of sand that pile up. Contemplate the silence, break the habits of a lifetime, enjoy your time away from the demands of a comfortable lifestyle. Go somewhere where there are no neighbors.

Hideaways are reassuring. The rough-hewn planks provide a simple yet effective screen against the noise and pollution of modern society. The hideaway is a haven, a bird's nest tucked away in the branches. Freed from the constraints of daily routine, life in a hideaway means having the time to stop and think, to watch the birds wheeling far above, to smell the wet grass, hear the wind singing in the branches and feel the roughness of the bark beneath one's fingers. Like a hermit in a cave or a wise philosopher in a Chinese tea pavilion, far from the strident demands of modern society, the owner of a hideaway comes there to seek peace, tranquillity, and wisdom, which he has grown unfamiliar with in the hubbub of his everyday surroundings. True isolation is fascinating. Poets and thinkers have for centuries sought refuge in retreats when looking for inspiration. At the dawn of the thirteenth century C.E., the Japanese poet Kamo No Chomei built himself a ten-foot-square hut on Mount Hino, near Kyoto, the former imperial capital. He fled Japanese society, which was undergoing a turbulent period, as the shoguns were in the process of taking over from the aristocracy and the country had recently suffered a series of natural disasters. Above all, he wanted to turn his back on the vanity of human society. He found peace in his hut of wood and thatch, comparing his life there to that of a silkworm that makes itself a cocoon as it grows old.

"Now hidden deep in the fastnesses of Mount Hino, I have put up eaves projecting on the south side to keep off the sun and a small bamboo veranda beneath them. On the west is the shelf for the offerings of water and flowers to Buddha, and in the middle, against the western wall is a picture of Amida Buddha so arranged that the setting sun shines from between his brows as though he were emitting his ray of light, while on the doors of his shrine are painted pictures of Fugen and Fudo. Over the sliding doors on the north side is a little shelf on which stand three or four black leather cases containing some volumes of Japanese poems and music and a book of selections from the Buddhist Sutras. Beside these stand a harp and a lute, of the kind called folding harp and jointed lute. On the eastern

Laurens' tree house is made of wood, in harmony with the surroundings. He has filled it with cushions to snuggle into, and a table where he can work, read, draw, or write, while listening to the creaking of the pine tree.

side is a bundle of fern fronds and a mat of straw on which I sleep at night. In the eastern wall there is a window before which stands my writing-table. A fire-box beside my pillow in which I can make a fire of broken brushwood completes the furniture. To the north of my little hut I have made a tiny garden surrounded by a thin low brushwood fence so that I can grow various kinds of medicinal herbs. Such is the style of my insubstantial cottage."

Men find comfort in small spaces, as if a small shelter gave better protection. As if a discreet, rustic hideaway were enough to guarantee peace of mind. It awakens faint memories of playing under a bed as a tiny child, jealously hoarding treasures in a place that we were sure no one would ever find. Hideaways are like a second skin, an outer layer of clothing over a coat. They are places where we can be utterly selfish, ban all compromises.

Hideaways calm the nerves by providing a sense of security. Although by definition they are designed to be ephemeral, they seem a permanent fixture from one century, and one continent, to another. Modest, ignoring the whimsical dictates of fashion, hideaways either

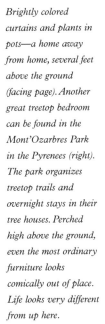

Brightly colored curtains and plants in pots—a home away from home, several feet above the ground (facing page). Another great treetop bedroom can be found in the Mont'Ozarbres Park in the Pyrenees (right). The park organizes treetop trails and overnight stays in their tree houses. Perched high above the ground, even the most ordinary furniture looks comically out of place. Life looks very different from up here.

resist change or adapt so that the changes fit their purpose. They are fixed points in our increasingly chaotic modern lives. In today's world, when one fashion sweeps in before the preceding trend has run its course, when every day another record scientific breakthrough is announced, when flexibility and adaptability are the new watch-words, hideaways seem more of an indispensable luxury than ever.

The master storyteller Italo Calvino wrote the quintessential tale of a man's need for a hideaway in his masterpiece *The Baron in the Trees*. This wonderful novel tells the story of Baron Cosimo Piovasco di Rondo, who decides at the tender age of twelve to give up life in society as a bad job and to live henceforth in the trees. From his vantage point perched in the branches, he can observe life with a coolly critical eye. Many admirers of the book have taken inspiration from Italo Calvino's tale, and set up home in the treetops.

In the maple forests of Maine and the splendid white oak forests of Oregon, from New Jersey to California, from Missouri to Massachusetts, people have begun building homes in the trees. Although still marginal, the movement is becoming more and more popular, as people look for an original way to make a break with the routine of their daily lives and cast their eyes upwards in search of inspiration. These hideaways have captured something of the pioneering spirit of the nineteenth-century settlers setting out to conquer virgin territory. Upmarket travel agencies in New York have long sold stressed-out executives weekend breaks in Maine and Vermont where they can go fishing and enjoy the simple life. In the 1970s, many people who were dissatisfied with the consumer society dropped out in search of an alternative lifestyle, living a simple life close to nature, without all the trappings of wealth. From Californian tree houses to Laura Ingalls Wilder's *Little House on the Prairie*, hideaways are an essential part of the American way of life, part of how the West was won. After all, Abraham Lincoln, one of America's greatest self-made men, was born in a log cabin, and ended up in the White House.

A crab fisherman in Eureka, California, lived his own version of the American Dream by building a series of astonishing hideaways in ocher and gray wood in the branches of gigantic redwoods hundreds of years old. They look like something out of a fairy tale, polished smooth by the wind and the sun. The hideaways seem to be attached to the branches of the giant sequoias by nothing more than a few threads. The stairs leading up to them curl around the vast trunks like tendrils of some fantastic creeper. Each hideaway houses a rickety-looking observatory with a few windows and a wood-fired stove. The fisherman designed them in memory of his son, drowned in a shipwreck in the 1970s.

Nowadays, wealthy American families are building luxuriously appointed homes in red American pine in the treetops. The designs are often inspired

by traditional American architecture, with upper floors, double roofs, screen doors, and verandas. In regions that are often prey to violent storms, even the most solid and well-built of these structures can be tossed around like sticks by the howling winds—nature's way of reminding us of the tale of the mighty oak and the fragile bulrush. The reed bent in the wind; the oak did not, and eventually its trunk snapped with the force of the wind.

Peter and Judy Nelson are mad about tree houses. In their work *The Treehouse Book*, they recount the strange tale of William Scott Scurlock, bank robber and mountaineer *extraordinaire*. Over ten years, he built a fabulous tower nearly thirty feet (nine meters) from the ground. His new home, set in a grove of Douglas firs near Olympia in Washington state, had three floors and a total surface area of 1500 square feet (140 square meters). From the outside, the building looked like a cross between a seashell and a mushroom. When the FBI took over the site after Scurlock's death, they found a cache of semi-automatic weapons, a collection of fake moustaches, and twenty thousand dollars in banknotes. In his treetop hideout, Scurlock had running water and electricity, a pulley system, trap doors, fire escapes, and a solarium. So it seems that the age of the highwayman lurking in the forest may not quite be gone forever!

The Strybing Arboretum in San Francisco has a modern version of the traditional American tree house. The groves of exotic tropical trees each bear proudly aloft a tree house designed by a leading architect. One particularly fine example, inspired by Far Eastern architecture, is called the Belly of the Koi. It is a crescent of red wood, some twenty feet (six meters) off the ground, in the branches of a eucalyptus with delicate pearl-gray bark.

A Frenchman called Alain Laurens shared the American dream of breaking with routine and looking down on the world around him. He built his perfect hideaway in the treetops. Tired of working fifteen hours a day for ten years, as his job as CEO of a large advertising agency demanded, his life was changed forever one day when he picked up an old copy of Calvino's *The Baron in the Trees*. He was seized with an irresistible desire to climb a tree and disappear in the foliage. As a child, he loved building fortresses out of cardboard boxes in his parents' apartment. At the age of fifty, he suddenly set about building a hideaway in an Aleppo pine on the farm where he would vacation in Bonnieux, in the Lubéron mountains

A comfortable office in the branches of an oak tree (left), and three hideaways built around ancient trees (facing page), all created by the Scottish-based company TreeHouse. The company has also worked on huts large enough to house entire conferences, seminars, and business lunches.

Twenty feet (six meters) above the ground in the branches of a venerable old maple in Connecticut, this tree house was built by the artist and architect John Ryman for the novelists Howard and Susan Kaminsky. The windows and door were reclaimed from older buildings, and the blinds are made of bamboo. This is where Howard, formerly CEO of Warner Books, dreams up the plots for his novels.

on the Mediterranean coast. He has constructed a delightful little home, around fifty square feet (five square meters), in red cedar, chosen because it is light and does not rot. The cottage is perched on a platform about twenty-five feet (eight meters) above the ground, and has unparalleled views of the surrounding forests, the Mont Sainte-Victoire, and the foothills of the Alps. The terrace is an invitation to while away the hours, sipping at an aperitif, eating the fat, black olives grown locally, hidden behind a screen of leaves. Alain Laurens does not let anyone into his private hideaway without permission: a little bell hangs from the roof of finely carved wood. There is even a basket on a rope to winch up supplies should Laurens decide to spend a few days without coming down to ground level. The young carpenter who worked on the hideaway was given strict instructions not to drive nails into the trunk of the tree. He came up with an ingenious system of metal links that encircle the trunk like a belt, resting on rubber strips to protect the bark. In this way the weight of the structure does not rest on the branches, while the staircase is held up by ropes. The hideaway has shaped itself to the tree, and not vice versa. And, like the tale of the oak and the bulrush, adapting to the forces of nature has proved the right choice. Alain Laurens' cabin in the trees has survived violent storms and tons of snow piled on the roof without damage.

Inside, there is nothing but a bench, a table, some cushions, and a few shelves for some favorite books. There is little to distract from the sighing of the wind in the pines and the scent of the resin. Laurens loves nothing more than to come here for a siesta or to read for an hour or two. He enjoys the extraordinary feeling of solitude, and waxes lyrical about the magic he senses all around him as he lies on his back, looking up through the carpet of leaves that cast a green light, so that he might be lying on the bottom of the ocean. He loves the feeling of being somewhere where no one has ever set foot before him, and says he can fully understand what drove men to try and conquer Everest. His passion for trees and tree houses has led him to embark on a new career. He quit his job at the advertising agency, and in 2000 founded a company specializing in tree-house design, *La Cabane Perchée*. One of his first commissions was a luxury 140-square-feet (13-square-meter) tree house in the suburbs of Paris for Yann Arthus-Bertrand, the photographer whose book *The Earth from the Air* has been a global success. The tree house is nearly forty feet (twelve meters) off the ground, and is equipped with solar panels. The elegant spiral staircase alone took a month to build. Soon after, Laurens was commissioned to build a hideaway inspired by Thai architecture in a copper beech in the grounds of a castle in Normandy.

These wealthy families could have spent their money on sports cars or a yacht. Instead, they chose to listen to their inner child. Alain Laurens says that often grandparents decide to build a tree house for their grandchildren, but end up succumbing to temptation in their turn and spending hours there, sipping an aperitif and watching the sun go down. Some families request particularly extravagant tree houses with roofs that open and even lightning conductors. Laurens is a little saddened by such requests. These are people who have failed to grasp that the essence of a hideaway is its simple, rustic, natural charm.

I find this hideaway mysterious. It looks like the first page of a photo-novel. The page that announces what is to come. The one where there is no one to be seen. The one where no one is speaking. My mother calls it the enticing page. All the elements of the plot are there on the first page, my mother says.

La Cabane d'Hippolyte, Marie Le Drian

A place to break with the past, a place of transition, halfway between the body and the house, a built object and yet a natural element—hideaways represent an unstable, creative equilibrium, an endless source of invention and poetry born of introspection and the feeling of being elsewhere, far removed from everyday life. Architects, thinkers, writers, artists, and even fashion designers have dreamed up some of their finest creations in hideaways, places of peace and inspiration. There, they can take a step back from the world and look at it in a different light, bringing a fresh vision to their work.

Claude Monet had a hideaway on the île aux Orties (Nettle Island), a tiny island near his home in Giverny, France. In fact, he bought the island so that he could paint there undisturbed, whatever the weather. Dylan Thomas had a writing hut made of blue planks, set in magnificent, wild landscape in western Wales, overlooking Carmarthen Bay. J.D. Salinger's daughter Margaret wrote in *Dream Catcher: A Memoir* how her father, author of the classic novel *The Catcher in the Rye*, would shut himself away in his very own hideaway, set in a clearing in a pine grove, at his home in Cornish, New Hampshire. At the end of a path overgrown with bushes and brambles, he had set up his "office," containing little more than a wood-fired stove, the back seat of a car to sit on, and a typewriter on a block of wood, where he would laboriously type his novels.

Today, several well-known fashion designers work in hideaways. The great *parfumeur* Serge Lutens has a hideaway nestled in a palm grove in Marrakech, where he draws inspiration for his fragrances from the scents of nature. The artist Patrick Serc shows his paintings and watercolors—inspired by the sea, his travels, and shelters made of driftwood—in a gypsy caravan in which he tours around the back lanes of Normandy. Not all of these hideaways are as plain as a monk's cell. Some of the artists bring the modern world with them, checking their email on their laptop on a rough-hewn wooden table. Technology and rustic simplicity can prove inspiring allies. . . .

Artists and poets have long sought refuge in hideaways to find the peace and quiet necessary to create their masterpieces. Dylan Thomas worked in a rough-and-ready hut in Wales (left), writing his poems on an untidy table (facing page, bottom). The Belgian artist Isabelle de Borchgrave paints and writes her delightful travel notebooks in her garden shelter (facing page, top). The structure was originally a beach hut, built on the dunes of the Belgian coast. She fell in love with it, and had it rebuilt in her garden in Brussels.

A country hideaway on the terrace of an apartment in the most elegant neighborhood in all Paris (left). A hut designed by Hugues Peuvergne, hidden away in a leafy copse (right). Whether in the heart of the city or the depths of the country, hideaways all share the same calm, soothing atmosphere.

Mary is an American who now lives in the heart of Paris. She has found room on her balcony for a hideaway, where she lets her imagination and her pen take flight. It is a most unusual place for a hideaway, in the heart of one of the most bustling neighborhoods in Paris.

The hideaway of reclaimed planks of wood, designed by the landscape architect Hugues Peuvergne, is eye-catching—if you happen to cast your glance upwards. Many people, of course, hurry past unaware of its existence. It is half-shrouded in vine leaves and decorated with wrought-iron bells. At night, candles glimmer through the windows.

When Mary takes us onto her balcony, we are in for quite a surprise. The hideaway is an illusion; there are just twenty-eight inches (seventy centimeters) from the front wall to the concrete wall of the apartment block. It is a magnificent piece of trompe-l'oeil. Although only a clever imitation of a garden shed, a mere façade, it is enough for Mary, a retired lecturer in oral literature, who spends many happy hours daydreaming and writing there. Here, in her tiny shelter, she finds the intimacy and privacy that she needs to write her books. Despite the noise of the street that floats up to her balcony, despite the all-pervading stress of city life, Mary can shut herself away and drift off to another, more playful world, where imagination reigns—something she found very difficult in her former office, where she was surrounded by books, telephones, faxes, reminders of a thousand and one things to do. Mary is writing a book on opera, and the theatricality of her little hideaway, which could almost be the scenery for a play, is an endless source of inspiration. The façade of the shelter, modestly hiding behind a veil of leaves, reminds Mary of a stage where nature plays out the acts of the seasons, and where she, as a writer, can project her own emotions. Thanks to her hideaway, tucked away under the vines, Mary has learned to look at art in a fresh light. She has decided to show the works of a friend of hers, inspired by Persian miniatures. She feels that in Paris, art has become a rather institutional affair, shut away in galleries and museums, and she wishes to reconnect with it on a more personal level.

The poetry of hideaways can be found in the most unexpected places. All you have to do is keep your eyes open, look upwards, and you will see little huts perched on balconies, splashes of imagination in the dull uniformity of urban architecture. One particular balcony that is worth looking out for near the extremely upmarket Place des Vosges in Paris regularly sprouts a hideaway every year to celebrate Sukkot, the Jewish Feast of Tabernacles in memory of the Hebrews' flight from Egypt and forty years wandering in the Sinai desert.

Many amateur do-it-yourself enthusiasts see building a hideaway as an ideal way of testing their own physical capacities, rediscovering their strength and the pleasure of working hard to create something themselves from start to finish. Sawing and hammering are excellent for getting rid of stress and putting trivial problems in perspective. People

who spend their entire working lives in front of a computer often long to get back in touch with their own bodies, so that even the blisters they get building their hideaway are a badge of pride. A number of farms and vacation camps now offer courses teaching stressed-out city executives how to build log cabins using nothing but an axe and their own brute strength. In a remote corner of southeastern France, high in the Alps, one entrepreneur—a former video game designer—has set up a company offering week-long courses in traditional South African building techniques. The course is popular with middle-aged CEOs who are keen to try a new challenge, a million miles from their day-to-day preoccupations. By learning to make a hut with their own hands, they rediscover how to interact with nature. In Oregon, the Out 'n' About tree house camp, in the midst of an oak forest, has a Tree House Institute which teaches visitors about life in the treetops, giving lessons on building tree houses and leading treetop expeditions.

In today's hi-tech, high-speed world, it is becoming clear to many people that technology is not the panacea it was heralded to be just a few decades ago. They are gradually rediscovering the charms of a low-tech lifestyle. And what could be more basic than a log cabin? Building your own hideaway is only partly about wanting to get in touch with a lost childhood dream. Part of the pleasure is the sheer pride of getting to grips with nails and planks and making something. It is not about virtual reality and concepts that become outdated in a matter of months. It is about learning ancestral skills passed down through the generations and putting together a real, three-dimensional, solid building.

The architect Philippe Le Moal decided to build his own hideaway when he found himself increasingly involved in plans and blueprints and losing touch with the building process, which had drawn him to architecture in the first place. He deplored the lack of imagination of the identikit garden sheds and imitation Swiss chalets that were all he could find on sale in his local garden center. With a friend, he set up a company, L'Île Instant, to design flat-pack garden sheds in wood and sheet metal, shaped like giant wheelbarrows, barges, and benches, playing with the notion of mobility. Resting on large wheels, the wheelbarrow design looks like it is waiting for someone to come and trundle it off. The barge shed seems to have become stranded on the lawn after a storm. Although the company was originally founded as a commercial venture to take advantage of a niche in the market, the two partners gradually became hooked, and test their latest imaginative designs in their own gardens.

It was a challenge for Le Moal to turn his back on the years spent studying architectural theory and actually get physically involved in the building process himself. He left behind a world of concepts, where the symbolism of the space was a vital factor,

The barge hut (left), with a large terrace, inspired by traditional Breton boats and designed by L'Île Instant, is perfect for an improvised summer party or for lazing in a deckchair under the stars, as is this fisherman's hut (right) on the shore of "Golden Pond," just north of the beach resorts of La Grande Motte and Carnon on France's Mediterranean coast. The owners come here to while away their Sunday afternoons, drinking pastis—the local aniseed tipple—and occasionally checking their rods.

This floating hut in Sweden (facing page) has hidden depths, like an iceberg. Visitors can spend a night in its underwater cabin. The twin beds are framed by large portholes, so that anyone staying there can contemplate the undersea world for hours on end. The hut on the right is designed by the company L'Île Instant.

where each design had to be approved by a panel of town planners. It was a real joy for him to rediscover a more intuitive approach to architecture. He shared with us his wish to return to the simpler building techniques of the nineteenth century. He believes that contemporary architecture is burdened with such complex materials, so few technical limitations, and such high expectations, that we have forgotten how to analyze buildings. He loves his sheds and hideaways because the traces of the building process are still visible in the finished construction. L'Île Instant's kits may be produced in factories and delivered in a flat pack, but each hut is certainly very unique.

The clients are encouraged to customize their purchase. One has developed the maritime theme of his barge shed, building masts and draping sails from them to hide the shed from prying eyes. Another has painted his shed in army camouflage colors. Others have turned the sheds into artists' studios or spare bedrooms where friends can stay all summer long. One shed has become the focal point of the garden. The children dress up inside before putting on plays for the grown-ups, and later on, as night falls, the adults dance on the decking. It is as if L'Île Instant provides their customers with the outline for a story, which they then build upon as they wish. It is a story that can be told over several decades.

In those days, we knew what the men got up to on Sundays. Games of shuffleboard were not forbidden on beaches. They went there, the men, down below the hideaway. The cider chilling in the stream that flowed beneath the hideaway. . . . The hideaway became a refreshment stand. They served cider there. Then wine. On St. John's Day, midsummer, they made love there. The wild hideaway. A place for night-time loving.

La Cabane d'Hippolyte, Marie Le Drian

51

Going further afield

I went to the woods because I wished to live deliberately, to front only the essential facts of life, and see if I could not learn what it had to teach, and not, when I came to die, discover that I had not lived.

Walden, H. D. Thoreau

Sometimes, a few hours are not enough. It can take more than a few moments of solitude to step back from life. The hideaway is no longer just a place to spend a sunny afternoon; it becomes a lifestyle choice, a clean break, a deliberate decision to live on the margins of a society that no longer corresponds to our needs and desires. People who choose to turn their backs on society like this live at a different speed, following nature's rhythms like Robinson Crusoe, or the rules of their new community. These hideaways bring us back to the child building a hideaway as a way of establishing his own rules. Choosing to live in a hideaway can be a subconscious act of resistance—humorous or obstinate, grandiloquent or modest, but an act of resistance all the same.

The American philosopher Henry David Thoreau is a hero to all those who wish to make a stand, however inadequate, against the creeping homogenization of society. In the mid-nineteenth century, as train tracks and telegraph poles were opening up the heart of this bold young nation, Thoreau turned his back on the birth of the modern world and chose to live in the pine and cedar forests of Massachusetts instead, a mile from his nearest neighbors. To awaken from his torpor, he felt the need to confront the forest and its animals. He built himself a cabin ten feet in length and fifteen feet wide. The roof was of planks with chamfered edges, the façade was of shingles. Here he led a frugal, solitary life, writing his masterpiece *Walden; or Life in the Woods*, a hymn in praise of nature. Thoreau spent his time bathing in his beloved Walden Pond, growing beans, and fishing. Even the mosquitoes that plagued him were a source of mystical wonder! He found the true meaning of life in this rediscovery of the world, in the contemplation of a frozen lake, or in the cries of owls. He relished the taste of freedom.

Other writers have repeated the experience. A century after Thoreau, the author Catherine Sanchez decided to spend a few years in a hideaway. She lived in a hut in the Carcans forest in southwestern France from 1976 to 1989, and wrote a book about her experiences. The book recounts the adventures of a group of artists who all lived in old shepherds' huts or shelters they made themselves within a couple of miles of her hideaway. She wrote, "Blessed was the time when society did not feel it to be its duty to exterminate such eccentrics." In their "miniature palaces" lost in the pine forests, the artists had water pumps in place of bathrooms, oil lamps for light, and snakes as roommates. Catherine Sanchez learned to love this solitude, feeling it made her a stronger person, far more aware of the secrets of nature. Her senses grew more acute; she could tell the birds apart by the

A hut in the stunning Adirondack mountains, in New York state (facing page). "The very simplicity and nakedness of man's life in the primitive ages imply this advantage, at least, that they left him still but a sojourner in nature." Walden; or Life in the Woods, H. D. Thoreau.

noise of their beating wings. She learned to appreciate the flash of light on the shiny varnished leaf of an arbutus, the valiant song of the robin, and to walk in the dark without fear. She despises the word *environment*, saying "it places man in the center of the world; being in my cabin taught me that man is not at the heart of life, but rather part of the great weave of the world." But the natural world taught her respect, and that freedom can only be obtained by following the rules of nature—rules as opposed to laws, coercion, or surveillance. The rules she learned to obey were the rhythm of the seasons, a deep respect for nature, silence and contemplation, and bowing to the angry wind or the tempestuous ocean, biting frost or searing heat. She writes: "Haunted, my modest habitation became a nest of visions, where imagination could develop in the constraints of daily life and be spurred on by them." After a few years of contemplation and creation, the artists moved on—some driven out by their fear of snakes, others by the building of a new golf course and the development of tourism in the region. These were signs of the arrival of an all-pervasive consumer society that left no room on its margins for eccentrics or dreamers: "Covetless—we were hardly in tune with the consumerist philosophy, we were reprehensible, subversive, sacrilegious! . . . And yet, we will all end up equal, in a box of four planks."

More and more landscape designers are choosing to include follies and huts in their garden designs. Garden centers are also selling more sheds, and made-to-measure garden hideaways designed by specialist architects are becoming increasingly popular. This hut on the shores of a lake (facing page) was designed by the Belgian company Kabane. This shelter (right) in the Venetian lagoon probably belongs to a hunter or angler.

Her way of resisting was to choose the rhythm of nature over frenzied consumerism, to prefer a camping stove to a microwave oven, to prefer contemplating sand-dunes to watching television. It was a daily program of resistance, made up of tiny details, yet radical in its impact. The hideaway is a fragile, permeable barrier between the soul and the universe, inside and outside. It makes it possible to enter into communion with nature, a talent we have often lost in the race for technological progress and the growth of urban sprawl. Today, nature is packaged, reshaped, blighted with wood-chip paths and signs telling us where to go and how not to get lost. Living in a hideaway means being scratched by brambles, getting sand in your eyes, and listening to the rain on the roof.

Each technological step forward, each announcement of another major scientific breakthrough, awakens in some people the urge to flee to a simpler place where nature and freedom are more than just words. This moment came four years ago for Sylvie Branellec. She had a good job in fashion, and lived in a large, sunny apartment in one of the best areas in Paris. She was so busy going about her daily routine that she had almost forgotten what lay beyond the boundaries of the city. Yet one day, she suddenly felt suffocated by this life and discovered an urgent need to question her priorities, to take a risk, to live something different. She had simply had all she could take of crowded trains, overheated offices, and the pressure of deadlines. She felt a weight lifting off her shoulders as she made the snap decision to throw it all in and make a clean break. She now lives in a one hundred and sixty-square-feet (fifteen-square-meter) hut in a forest outside Paris. Her friends laughingly compare it to their own garden sheds, where they store their gardening

shoes and winter coats. But Branellec has never been happier. Together with a friend who ran a carpentry firm, she made the hut fit to live in. Today, it is charming, with ivy growing up the walls, a mezzanine, a large window, and electricity. The walls are of wood, and the floor is thickly carpeted. There can be no more welcoming place on a cold winter's afternoon when the snow lies thick on the ground. Branellec lives there all year round, entirely in tune with nature. After the great storm that struck France in December 1999, she lived by candlelight. Three trees were blown down nearby, but fortunately her hideaway was not damaged. The following year, there were floods. Water crept in through the electrical circuitry. Every year, she watches the leaves turn brown and fall from the trees. Every winter, she sits out the storms, listening to the shrieking wind and the pelting rain. And every spring, she watches the new buds burst through their leathery cases. The rhythm of the seasons, the incessant cycle of life, give her an impression of nature's magic strength. She can sense the physical energy of the sap forcing its way to the very tips of the leaves. This solitude has given her boundless self-confidence. She now spends her time designing and making jewelry and photo montages for sale in her shop in Paris. She has learned to be at peace with herself and others, far from the aggressive rush of life in any major city. Her hut gives her the silence and the time she needs to draw on her deep sources of creativity.

Branellec takes us to visit her hut following a well-defined ritual. She never drives through town, preferring the longer road across the fields of bright yellow, oily-scented rape. She tells us proudly of the way people around her reacted to her announcement. The ones who called her crazy have now grudgingly admitted that this new life has done her a lot of good. She also tells us how she overcame her initial fears. "To begin with, I deliberately forced myself to go out and walk round the hut every time I got scared, so as not to let the fear take over. Over the months, I got used to all the little sounds of the forest. I find the fact that the space is so small incredibly reassuring: I'm never scared that someone might be lurking in the next room!" Branellec is also very proud of the fact that she is different from everyone else, that she dared to make the break and find her freedom. "In this doll's house hidden in the woods, like the gingerbread cottage in Hansel and Gretel, I feel like I rule the world! Living in a hideaway is a step backward, but it is perfectly counterbalanced by the freedom I now enjoy." She can light fires whenever she feels like it, can sleep with the doors open, change the carpets as often as she fancies. In a space of a hundred and sixty square feet, everything is simpler. All the furniture she collected in her former life in Paris is now outside. Her dining room table and chairs are covered in snow in winter. She loves this sense of utter liberty.

Laurence Nicolas has written a book about the anarchic architecture in the village of Beauduc in the Camargue, a few miles north of the Mediterranean coast. She writes that while it all seems to be falling apart at the seams, it is in fact obeying a new kind of logic—the logic of the hideaway that puts together scavenged and recycled building materials like pieces of a jigsaw puzzle, not necessarily creating the picture on the box, but perhaps one that is more interesting. Not every person who drops out of the rat race in search of inner

Twenty minutes from Bordeaux, L'Île aux Oiseaux (Bird Island), a group of buildings on piles, forms part of the Sources de Caudalie vinotherapy center. Set in the heart of the Graves wine region outside Bordeaux, each hut is wholly given over to the physical and spiritual well-being of the guests. The wooden walls of the bedrooms (left) and the peaceful sound of the waves lapping against the piles create an atmosphere of perfect peace.

peace chooses to live alone in the forest. For every solitary soul living in splendid isolation, there is a group of convivial, like-minded people living in harmony. Their homes may be rough-and-ready, but there is a real sense of solidarity and warmth. Together they form a tightly-knit clan, far removed from the anonymity of city life. They follow the same rules, the same values, and each family is on an equal footing. There are no hierarchies here. A few decades ago, such villages of huts and rudimentary shelters were home only to anglers, oyster fishermen, and a few eccentrics. Now people are looking at them with renewed interest. They offer a lifestyle in harmony with the environment, a chance to learn age-old traditions that have died out elsewhere; they are a space of liberty in a world of building regulations and planning permission. They resist where other villages have succumbed to encroaching urbanization and the lure of income from tourists.

The village of Gruissan in southern France, near the Pyrenees, is a fine example. There are about one thousand chalets, all built by the locals using whatever materials they could find—planks of wood and sheets of corrugated iron. The first chalets sprang from the sand almost overnight at the tail end of the nineteenth century. The first builders were wealthy merchants and wine growers from the nearby town of Narbonne. The village grew rapidly in the 1930s when the first bus service arrived in the village. However, all but one of the chalets were destroyed by the German army in 1943. After the war, they were rebuilt, again using whatever was available—steel, sheet metal, train carriages. Since then, Gruissan has been famed for its relaxed holiday atmosphere. It is perhaps less comfortable than the nearby seaside resorts, but it certainly has more character.

A hundred miles further east, along the Mediterranean coast, are the famous fishermen's huts in the *calanques*—limestone creeks—round Marseilles. The villages of Les Goudes and La Verrerie are especially picturesque, with blinding white cliffs plunging into emerald green water. The huts huddled on the slopes of the creeks were once synonymous with the hard labor of the fishermen who plied these treacherous coasts, but are now more associated with *farniente*, siestas, pastis—the local aniseed tipple—and a rich, steaming bowl of bouillabaisse, a fish stew. Space in the creeks is at a premium, and sitting with one's feet dangling in the water as one sips an aperitif is now a costly hobby.

Beauduc, near Arles in the Camargue, is home to fishermen, dropouts in search of solitude, and families who have fallen under the spell of the Camargue flatlands that seem to stretch on forever, broken only by tufts of samphire around the lagoons. Robinson Crusoe would have felt at home here. Set in the heart of the plains of sand, between two salt-water inlets, the unkempt village has a fascinating, almost ghostly atmosphere. The dilapidated huts and caravans seems to have been abandoned here, at the ends of the earth. The main road stops dead. A rutted track leads off to the right. A couple more miles, and the tarmac surface gives way to dirt. We slow down, driving carefully in second gear, trying to avoid the worst of the potholes. After a while, it seems safer just to let the wheels follow the ruts that zigzag along

the track. At the end of the track we come to a broad stretch of gray sand—and the village of Beauduc. Most of the huts and caravans are huddled together, but a few stand apart, on the patches of higher ground. The shelters seem to have been thrown together in great haste—although we know that some have been standing for decades—and it looks as if the least puff of wind will blow them over. The walls are aslant, and the lopsided roofs mimic the uneven lines of the horizon and the waves of the sea. The huts in Beauduc look like they were built from giant Meccano sets, with bits added here and there as the family

The village of Beauduc in the Camargue, a region famed for its lakes and lagoons, is an unusual sight. All the homes are caravans or huts made of recycled building materials such as plates of corrugated iron and plastic sheeting. Here, far from the nearest town, where the only roads are dirt tracks, eccentricity is a virtue, and happy-go-lucky, topsy-turvy buildings the order of the day.

expanded. One part of a wall might be made of sheets of corrugated iron, while another might be made of weather-beaten planks from a nearby saltworks. The shutters might have come from a house recently demolished in the vicinity, with plastic sheeting in the place of window panes. Some of the older dwellings have a wall or two in concrete. Each is topped with a stovepipe poking from the roof and has its own rainwater tank. Some are decorated with huge whale vertebrae washed up on the beach after a spring storm, or with evocatively shaped driftwood "sculptures." A few have wooden fences or roped-off gardens—valiant attempts to stake a claim to a corner of this endless expanse of beach, of dunes scattered with samphire plants, dark, brackish lagoons, and white streaks of salt across the sand, as far as the eye can see.

The charmingly anarchic spirit of this village is clearly visible in the "hideaways of a place between two worlds," as the sociologist Bernard Picon calls them. He is especially interested in the way the inhabitants collect anything and everything, hoarding their finds like magpies, blissfully ignorant of the esthetic norm. Some of the huts are shockingly ugly. Many of them are beautiful despite—or maybe because of—their chaotic structure. Their fragile appearance belies their solidity. Once inside, the huts are as warm and welcoming as any home, despite the wind whistling down the stovepipe. The owners often have a lifetime's collection of ornaments, fishing gear, hurricane lamps, and barometers on display. Some of the houses have been converted from old train carriages from the local line. Others are just a caravan up against a lean-to of old planks, or several caravans bumper to bumper, their leaking roofs patched up with Camargue reeds. The most intriguing hut is without doubt the one belonging to a man known only as The Indian, one of Beauduc's most famous residents. He lives in a refuge on piles, more like a fortress than a home, topped with a weather-vane and solar panel, a giant poster of Che Guevara, and a tortoise shell. As visitors began to arrive in Beauduc, The Indian felt the need to get even further away, so he built himself a fabulous floating pontoon where he could retire for the duration of the vacation season. It is a caravan on a raft, with its own solarium, decorated with reeds. Although the homes here seem to be set down in a casual, haphazard manner, the villagers do in fact have a strict

In the Caroux mountains, part of the Cévennes chain to the north of the Mediterranean city of Montpellier, a hermit moved from his native Germany to set up home in an ingenious wooden hut of his own design. He lives high in the Cévennes, drawing water from the mountain torrents, far from the nearest traces of modern civilization.

hierarchy depending on how long they have lived there. The standing of each family in the hierarchy is shown in how far advanced the work on their home is, and which part of the bay it is in. The oldest homes, which are the most elaborate, are in Beauduc Village. These families were the pioneers. The northern side is home to the second generation, whose homes are more rough-and-ready. The most recent arrivals, who often do not stay very long, live in Beauduc Beach. Their homes are little more than caravans, making it easier for them to move on as they wish. Many of the people who live in Beauduc have full-time jobs as welders, rail workers, craftsmen, fishermen, or shopkeepers. Some just come for the weekend, while others live here all year round. Yet despite their differences, they are all united in their rejection of a run-of-the-mill, conformist life. They all want to experience something off the beaten track, whether it is just for a weekend or a few months. Sometimes they come for a few weeks and stay for a lifetime. They grow to prize the taste of freedom and the joy of setting their own limits.

The ethnologist Laurence Nicolas first went to Beauduc out of professional interest. She fell in love with the village and has now been living there for four years. She says, "Beauduc is a question of attitude, almost like a religion. It has its 'thou shalt nots' like any other religion. The first commandment in the Beauduc bible is to live in direct contact with nature." The people of Beauduc physically confront their natural surroundings on a daily basis. They eat what nature provides: chickens scratching in the sandy yards; *tellines*, a type of shellfish found only in the vicinity; snails gathered in the gray light of early morning; and home-grown asparagus. Locally, the people of Beauduc are known as "the beachcombers." Many of them do spend a lot of time combing the beach, looking for any jetsam that might have washed up and that they can find a use for. They know that Beauduc will not give them an easy life. It is searingly hot in summer, and in winter the wind howls through the cracks in the walls. Fresh water is also scarce. Some of the children who grew up here cannot wait to turn their backs on it and experience the bright lights of city life. But for most, life in Beauduc means utter freedom. Some children leave the village to study, only to return every vacation to enjoy the water sports and eventually to celebrate their graduation with riotous parties. It is a place that welcomes transgression.

The very existence of Beauduc is somehow gleefully subversive. It represents a sort of vacuum, an unreal place where the normal rules of society—all the more rigid for being unspoken—do not apply. The people of Beauduc believe rules are made to be stretched, if not broken. They have created a microcosm where conviviality, not conformity, reigns. Small favors, such as mending a lawnmower, are repaid with a bottle of cool, refreshing aniseed pastis. That evening, the two families will spend hours talking over an aperitif. While the children gradually nod off and are carried to bed, the adults mull over hunting trips, discuss the best places to find wild mushrooms, and boast about the latest sardine catch. Here, clothing is not seen as a way of indicating social status. It is unheard-of to knock before visiting a neighbor. Laurence Nicolas concludes: "There is no clear distinction between inside and outside, between the public and private domains." She writes: "The confines of Beauduc seem to have a symbolic function, in many ways similar to the role of the forest in folk tales." She also evokes "the sense of oblivion, the return to the wild, and the freedom that a stay in this village of hideaways engenders. . . . So it is hardly surprising to find there communities

on the fringes of the law, or that themes of disorder and inversion—the spirit of carnivals, festivities, and unbridled playfulness—should be to the fore."

It would be unthinkable to try and impose normal rules and planning regulations on Beauduc. When the local authorities block access to the beach for caravans, the people of Beauduc invent highly inventive strategies to find a way around them. As early as the mid-eighteenth century, Beauduc was a fishing village of huts built of stone and lime. The land was taken over by saltworks in the 1930s, which were destroyed in their turn during World War II. After the war, the land was reclaimed by the workers from the saltworks, who scavenged old building materials and equipment—corrugated iron, plastic sheeting, caravans, old train carriages. Since the 1950s, the village has been a thorn in the side of the powers that be and the local population, who see Beauduc as nothing more than an illegal and unsightly eyesore on a beautiful stretch of coastline. The village has held out thus far, but its future is far from safe.

Beauduc's defiance of the planning laws is symptomatic of the way hideaways flirt with illegality. In our society, which hands down laws and regulations on every aspect of life, it is refreshing to think that hideaways owe their charm precisely to the fact that they manage to slip through the net of the law. When hideaways are given legal recognition, their owners set about making them more solid and permanent. What was a hideaway becomes a house. Beauduc has so far avoided this trap. Bernard Picon says, "They defy all attempts to classify them, and do not belong in any network. They resist the tide of isolation that cuts people off in their own homes, stand up to the market economy, and reject the idea that interpersonal relations should be based solely on what the other person can do for us. Hideaways unite people. They reunite concepts that our society sees as distinct categories, such as work and leisure, childhood and adulthood, production and consumption, the built and the non-built. Hideaways are a joyful departure from a rational categorization of the world."

The mere presence of these ragtag constructions on a piece of land is enough to mark it out as a space where the normal rules governing society do not apply—scraps of land where people still enjoy a gregarious lifestyle have long since vanished in our modern cities. Hideaways bring together people who would otherwise never have had a chance to meet. In Beauduc, for example, the start of summer is heralded by the arrival of hordes of visitors curious to discover this mythical village and its inhabitants, uncompromising in their rejection of the trappings of material wealth. The old fishermen find themselves rubbing shoulders with well-known photographers and famous personalities come to taste the bohemian lifestyle for the weekend—there are signed photos pinned up in the local fish restaurants.

It is becoming a problem in many rural areas that all of the old buildings—shepherds' huts in the Scottish Highlands, farm laborers' cottages in the east of England, even abandoned train stations—are being acquired as weekend and vacation homes, driving up prices and thus squeezing out young local families and gradually draining all the vitality out of the community. While it is preferable that such homes should be restored by wealthy weekenders rather than simply abandoned, it is comforting to know that places like Beauduc resist.

Each country and each region has a typical style of hut that reflects the local environment, rural customs, architectural traditions, and available building materials (wood, stone, wattle and daub, or even corrugated iron). This pigeon loft in the Pyrenees (left) is now used by hunters as a blind. Facing page: a typical Provençal borie, *or circular dry-stone hut.*

Another potential danger facing the free and easy lifestyle represented by Beauduc is that our consumer society, having detected a market for it, will simply package it and sell it like any other commodity, presenting it as a kind of folk museum rather than the vibrant, living community it is today. The people who share the Beauduc ideal are struggling against this encroaching tide, trying to preserve a sense of authenticity, and distinguishing between tourists visiting for the weekend, recent arrivals come to stay, and long-term residents. France's Atlantic coast provides an interesting case in point. Each stretch of the hundreds of miles of coastline has its own traditional style of hut, from the long, thin buildings on piles in the Gironde estuary in the south, to the square bulk of the oyster-fishermen's huts on the Île d'Oléron and La Tremblade further north, and the pontoons built out over the river Charente. Yet whatever the differences in style, each of these regions is facing the same difficulty: how to balance the needs of the few remaining fishermen and the hordes of tourists in search of relaxation and pure sea air. This problem is older than might

Beach huts were invented in the early nineteenth century, when sea bathing was all the rage. Handed down from generation to generation, they are delightful places to spend a long, lazy summer's day. Their fortunate owners return year after year to catch up on the news, play cards, or just watch the world go by. Beach huts in Bernières-sur-Mer in the Calvados region of Normandy (right) are used for storing parasols and deckchairs, as are these brightly colored beach huts in the region of Cape Town, South Africa (left).

at first be thought. In the early twentieth century, along the coast from Saint Nazaire, famous for its shipyards, well-heeled local merchants began to take over the traditional fishermen's huts, which were built out at sea, on piles, with long, narrow gangplanks leading back to the shore. One hundred years on, and several generations later, the huts still belong to the same families.

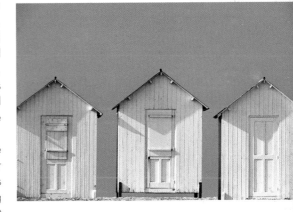

For generations, the village of L'Herbe in the Bassin d'Arcachon relied on oyster fishing for its income. Nowadays, the huts on the beach are decorated with hanging baskets, valiant attempts to disguise the fact that the walls are worn and bleached by the wind and the sand. The huts are almost touching each other; their roofs overlap. Most of the outer walls are made of planks of pine nailed vertically to the structure, a technique imitated from the huts built by resin-tappers in the great pine forests planted in the southwest of France in the eighteenth century. The planks have acquired a soft sheen, polished by the joint action of the sun and the salt, blackened by the wind. There are fishing nets and hollyhocks in the tiny gardens. Walls with a dignified gray patina stand side by side with jaunty-looking huts, freshly painted in bright hues of pale pink or emerald green. The roofs of the oldest huts are clumped with moss and stained with lichen. The owners have added extensions over the years, so that each hut is unique. One has a roof shaped like the letter W; another has an extraordinary neo-Gothic awning. Nearby is a hut with a double sloping roof and, next to that, one on piles, which seems to look down on its neighbors with a sneer.

When the huts were first built in the 1880s, they were very basic—just four walls and a roof, roughly twenty feet long and twelve feet wide (six by four meters). They were used for storing equipment and sheltering in case of sudden storms. Over the decades, the huts have been enlarged. In some, the posts indicating the limits of the zone where building was

permitted are now in the middle of the kitchen! We visited one hut where a portrait of the current owner's grandfather, a customs officer, has been given pride of place. The walls are now leaning at such an odd angle that the owner had to have slanting window frames specially made to fit in them. Traces can still be seen in the sitting room of the original hut, built by the owner's great-grandfather, an oyster fisherman. It was half as big as the structure is today.

There are still a few oyster fishermen living in the villages of L'Herbe, Le Piraillan, and Le Canon. Each hut has a wealth of family memories going back generations. The old folk like to tell the story of how their grandparents came to settle here in the mid-nineteenth century. They originally lived in the villages of La Teste and Andernos on the opposite side of the bay, and sailed across to fish in these waters abounding in fish. If they were caught in bad weather, they would sleep on the shore in their overturned boats. Today, only one of these overturned hulks survives; the rest were replaced over the years by rudimentary huts. The fishermen would sail back to their villages on the other side of the bay at neap tide. The huts were the first signs of colonization on this side of the bay. It is difficult to imagine the dangers faced by the fishermen in those early days. Nowadays, the village is a sunny, welcoming place, overrun by tourists every summer. Nevertheless, the residents who live here all year round are proud of their seagoing heritage. The gulf between them and the recent arrivals who come down here for the weekend will be very difficult to bridge.

In the 1920s and 1930s, the playwright and film director Jean Cocteau, the actor Jean Marais, and the poet Max Jacob would regularly come and stay in one of the huts that had neither electricity nor running water. Cocteau was fond of comparing the scenery with the great open landscapes of Texas. The old folk still talk of the village fetes that are now nothing but a distant memory. The only reminders of the old way of life are the games of *boules* that the old men play on the beach. This nostalgia is the same in rural villages all over Europe, but it is perhaps stronger in this village of rough-and-ready, yet sturdy, huts, remnants of a vanished world. The huts, mute witnesses of several lifetimes of hard labor, seem at odds with the new wave of tourists. Many have been bought up by wealthy families from Bordeaux who come here for the weekend or a month or two over the summer, to sip an aperitif on the beach as the sun goes down, or maybe to spend a day out in a boat with one of the old fishermen. The famous architects and fashion designers who have a holiday home here deliberately leave the dusty roads full of potholes to discourage visitors. One lawyer who built a home that his neighbors judged to be too flashy and out of keeping with the character of the place was banned. It seems that these wealthy owners like to keep their bohemian playground private and exclusive, so that they can play at living the simple life—for a few weeks. They pay a fortune to acquire these huts that are—in principle at least—only for sale or rent to fishermen. Yet however superficial this attraction for the simple life, it does have the virtue of making the new owners of these hideaways question their comfortable lifestyle and their own ideals, if only for a short while. For example, Bordeaux has the reputation of being a rather stiff, formal city. In their weekend

The owners of this hut on a jetty in the Gironde region in the southwest of France have called their home away from home Paradise. Many such huts have been acquired in recent years by vacationers looking for somewhere they can return to time and time again with the same delight. Who would not like to wake up in the morning with such a fabulous view over Saint Nazaire bay?

"Here, I can live simply, in my hut that is so happy and so rich." The playwright, novelist, and film director Jean Cocteau owned a hut in the oyster-fishing village of Piquey on the Bassin d'Arcachon. Now, nearly a hundred years later, the villages strung like beads along the bay are home to fishermen, tourists, and city-dwellers hoping to get away from it all and lead a simple life in the open air.

hideaways, the atmosphere is more relaxed. People feel free to drop in unannounced for drinks, and T-shirts and shorts are the order of the day. They spend the weekend working on their skiff under the watchful eyes of a pair of egrets, or collecting whelks in the oyster beds. Today, half of all the homes in the villages in Cap Ferret belong to weekend visitors.

The local authorities have now taken the situation in hand. There is now a bylaw stating that the huts are reserved exclusively for fishermen and oyster farmers. There is also an extremely restrictive set of architectural guidelines: the floor surface must not exceed 775 square feet (72 square meters), there must not be any upper floors, the colors and building materials must be approved before construction—down to the degree at which the roofs slant and the style of the roof tiles (which must be given a special patina designed to make them look weathered). The mailboxes must be cased in wood. These efforts to protect this unique architectural heritage are laudable, but also sadly revealing. It is a shame that the huts have to be protected like an endangered species. They are little more than museum pieces. Such rules and regulations are anathema to the spirit of the hideaway, which is precisely the opposite—a lively, innovative, personal vision of architecture. The only people who still have the skills necessary to preserve these huts are building contractors. The intuitive skills of the men who built the huts from overturned boats have been lost. There is no spark of spontaneity in the process. As the ethnologist Marie-Dominique Ribéreau-Gayon says, "The pastel colors do not correspond to the historical tradition of these huts, which were originally mostly black, because they were tarred and coated in oil to keep away parasites. They are restored to become small, cute, and charming, like the cottage of the seven dwarves in the forest. The rules are turning these huts into the archetypal child's dream hideaway."

The hideaway spirit has become a brand, taken up by architects and advertising executives. Naomi Klein's book *No Logo* details how the Canadian firm Roots has developed its own take on the phenomenon: "In April 1999, the Roots Lodge wasn't yet open, but construction was far enough along to make the concept perfectly clear: a high-end, fully branded summer camp for adults. Instead of canoes, an 'adventure station' rents out ocean kayaks and surfboards; instead of outhouses, each cabin has its own hot tub; instead of the communal campfire, individual gas fireplaces. The rough-hewn wooden cabins are equipped with the entire Roots home furniture line." Back in the region of L'Herbe, the latest real estate developments are imitations of traditional resin-tappers' huts right by the beach. The real versions are all further inland, in the pine forests. One shopping mall in the suburb of Bordeaux planned its business strategy around the image of fishermen's huts as a way of tapping into the strong feeling of local identity. Even banks and department stores have begun to use the image of huts as shorthand for friendly, local service. It remains to be seen whether their non-conformist spirit will survive being exploited for commercial purposes.

He remembers that the bells of freedom rang as loudly in his head as the wind, and that finally he found himself back at home: wooden walls, sand all around a small space invaded by the crashing of the ocean. His home: the only habitat that truly suited him, which fitted him like a suit worn for thousands of years, which expanded him until he was pushed into unbounded exultation.

En Cabanes, Catherine Sanchez

Elsewhere

Some dwellings are marvelous. I never wanted to stay long in any of them. I was in constant fear of doors that shut, traps. Cells that close down over the mind. The nomad's life is the shepherd's. . . . Nathaniel, I was sometimes detained by the strangest lodgings. There were some in the middle of forests; some on the water's edge; some that were very spacious. But as soon as familiarity made me cease to notice them, as soon as I was no longer astonished by them, no longer drawn by the promise of their windows and was on the verge of beginning to think, I left them.

Fruits of the Earth, Book 6, André Gide, tr. Dorothy Bussy.

Who never dreamed as a child of running away in a gypsy caravan? The artist Patrick Serc has decorated his caravan with quotations from Treasure Island. *His art is inspired by the sea and the modest fisherman's huts he sees on his travels.*

Rooted to the ground, yet precarious. One puff of wind would be all it took to float away, to begin all over again, somewhere new, at the bottom of the garden or on another continent. Hideaways are redolent with adventure, danger, and exoticism. They represent the call of the wild, the lure of the nomadic lifestyle.

Jean-Louis Etienne says, "Hideaways are a lifestyle choice, a way of escaping the fear of responsibility and burdens that tie you down and imprison you. Stones and concrete represent a serious, grown-up investment, whereas hideaways are light, mobile, ephemeral." Temporary and adaptable almost by definition, hideaways symbolize movement and mobility. Whether not quite finished or not yet dismantled, hideaways are the very antithesis of certainty and immobility. They offer freedom of movement, like a second skin. Hideaways are about adventure, not putting down roots, flexibility, not heavy obligations. Caravans are a crystallization of the pioneering spirit of the hideaway. They represent the desire to flee the burdensome worries of daily life—who did not dream, as a child, of running away to join the circus? Nowadays, top-class hotels sell a taste of the bohemian lifestyle in the form of overnight stays in gypsy caravans. For the less affluent, mobile homes have never been so popular. Even if they never travel further than a neighboring field, they hint at a longing for adventure. There is something magical about stepping into a caravan. It is like the first step of a journey that could last a lifetime. The thrillingly adventurous Romany lifestyle has become a myth, thanks to works like *Carmen* and *The Barefoot Contessa*, although modern-day travelers find it increasingly difficult to lead their traditional wandering lifestyle. Jeanne Bayol and her partner Jean-Marie live in Saint-Rémy-de-Provence, in the south of France. The couple are fascinated with gypsy culture; their pleasantly shady garden is crowded with caravans of different shapes and sizes, in various states of repair. Bayol has noted that her clients all share a need to feel they have a private, intimate place to seek refuge. Her caravans make perfect hideaways. She says: "Every time you enter a caravan, a new story washes over you." She has made it her life's work to keep this ancient nomadic culture alive by renovating the caravans she buys all over Europe from gypsies who have given up traveling. Her latest

Caravans are increasingly popular, with their evocations of the wild, free, romantic Romany lifestyle. Many hotels now offer overnight stays in gypsy caravans parked in the grounds, as here in Provence.

project is a 1920s Pont du Château—the Rolls Royce of caravans—which still has its original wooden friezes on the sides. She is repainting it in bright, sunny colors. The interior is already decorated with velvet curtains, bright pink cushions brought back from India, porcelain figures, and Chinese lanterns. Bayol has also added an old wood-burning stove she bought at a yard sale, bringing an ambience of warmth even when it is not lit. As was traditional in this style of caravan, the parents' bed is built in above the children's bed, which has doors that are shut at night. The gypsy caravans Bayol buys are generally very basic. The ones she buys from fairground stall holders are much more elaborately decorated: on occasion, she has come across marble basins and superb gilt mirrors. Some caravans are all in wood, while others have walls of sheet metal and a tarred roof with a stovepipe sticking out. Bayol finds a corner in all of the caravans she renovates for a small altar and pictures of Hindu gods as a reminder of the Indian origins of the Romany people. She has a special fondness for bead curtains and splashy colors such as purple, yellow, and turquoise. The result can be a little over the top and kitsch, but that is the way Bayol likes it, precisely because a caravan is not a house. It is a place for daring to try out the most extravagant and whimsical decorations. Again, we find the theme of transgression—daring to rebel against the tyranny of good taste. One of Bayol's favorite projects was an old caravan full of bullet holes, which she sold to a flamboyant Swiss flamenco dancer, who came to collect it in a brand new convertible. The dancer has set the caravan up in her garden in a well-heeled suburb of Geneva, and uses it to practice her latest choreographies, much to the horror of the neighbors! Bayol says, "People with a passion for caravans often have an ambivalent attitude, a mixture of fascination and apprehension. They fall for the clichés about travelers—that they are all poets, barefoot beauties like Esmeralda from *The Hunchback of Notre Dame*, dancers with their arms covered in jangling bracelets, or chicken thieves. The unknown is always a little scary." Some of Bayol's most enthusiastic clients have been city-dwellers, who felt something was missing from their lives. "Caravans fulfill a need for cosmopolitanism. They might have been all over the world, sold on from family to family. They are a heady blend of east and south, the films of Emir Kusturica and flamenco, the pink and turquoise of the Slavs and the red of the Mediterranean."

Imagine exploring a whole range of different countries and cultures while enjoying all the comforts of your own home. A caravan means having private space, but no roots, no ties. It is an age-old dream. In 1926, the eccentric writer and inventor Raymond Roussel came up with a design for what he called a "nomad villa"—a combination caravan and automobile with all the creature comforts. A journalist reporting on the design wrote: "It is impossible to imagine a more agreeable way to travel, or one that is richer in new sensations, than one that allows us to greet the day wherever our whim dictates . . . yet without giving up a single one of our habits, still enjoying all the advantages of the family home—in short, tasting the unique satisfaction of traveling without leaving home." In Roussel's

design for his nomad villa, the sitting room could be transformed into a bedroom, with an ingenious fold-up bed. He planned it to be safe at the high speed (for those days!) of twenty-five miles (forty kilometers) an hour. The journalist was clearly impressed: "In days to come, 'nomad villas' will throng the world's roads, bringing back, in a more luxurious form, the long-gone days of tribes of herders and the era now drawing to a close of wandering Zingari [gypsies], unapologetic lovers of nature, of the open air, and of utter freedom beneath the sky."

Such mobile hideaways are a common sight on America's roads. They have become part of the American myth, rooted in the pioneering tradition which saw roads as a symbol of freedom. From the covered wagons of the first families to go West, to the anonymity of the Greyhound buses that crisscross the continent, the tradition of pushing back the frontiers of personal experience is part of America. Today, John Wayne fans can still set out to explore Wyoming in a wagon straight off the set of a classic Western. The fashion designer Ralph Lauren recently auctioned off his collection of Airstreams, the comfortable aluminum trailers that were a familiar sight across America in the 1930s. Each was decorated in a different style inspired by the American dream, in themes inspired by Westerns or by nature. Other less well-known designers have come up with their own variation on the caravan. One fine example is the Tumbleweed, a strange hybrid of a mobile home and a traditional log cabin. The Tumbleweed came about when its inventor decided to avoid the planning laws by adding wheels to his home. It is classic American architecture, with a pointed roof, an arched window, and a canopy above the door. It looks almost surreal towed behind its owner's station wagon! Just one hundred and thirty square feet (twelve square meters) in size, it contains everything the designer needs, and is environmentally friendly: a wood-burning stove, cupboards and shelves on every inch of the walls, a compost toilet, and a solar-powered television. Some people have gone further afield in search of inspiration, to central Asia, where nomads live in round tents called yurts. These magnificent structures are made of wood, cloth, and animal skins. Their circular shape is said to be restful, and the sense of sharing in an age-old tradition is deeply soothing. In Asia, the yurt's round shape is a symbolic reference to the universe and the elements. The structure is extremely light and easy to maneuver, yet solid. They are designed for use on all sorts of terrain. Hal Wynne-Jones, a businessman from Gloucestershire, once spent a night in a yurt in Anatolia. He never forgot how wonderful it was, and decided to start a business making yurts back home in England. He plaits wands of hazelnut to form the round walls, bending them inwards and tying them at the top for the roof. He then throws a gigantic sheet of canvas over the structure. He sells his yurts for use as garden sheds, tents for festivals, concerts, and weddings, and even as saunas.

Mongolian yurts are dark and cozy, with a reassuringly solid circular wooden frame. In Mongolia, this form represents the universe. This yurt (left) was made in Paimpont, in Brittany. At Hill Lodge in Senegal the rooms are in the powerful branches of baobab trees (facing page). It is a perfect place to meditate.

Matusadona Water Lodge is built on Lake Kariba, downstream from the Victoria Falls in Zimbabwe. This enchanting lodge is all in pine, eucalyptus, and teak. It can only be reached by canoe. The heating and electricity are solar-powered, and food supplies and mail are delivered by taxi-plane.

Many travelers today are fed up with the sameness of hotels in major cities all over the world, and are looking for something a bit different. One of the first and most unusual businesses to dare something different was the Treetops Hotel in Kenya, where Princess Elizabeth was staying in 1952 when she became Queen Elizabeth II. Her room was perched forty feet up in the branches of a giant fig tree in the Aberdare National Park. Nowadays, there are many more of these unusual hotels, in the jungle or in the heart of the desert, beloved of travelers who are looking for something more than the blandness of the international hotel chains, who are willing to pay the price to see the last few unspoiled wildernesses before they in turn are opened up to hordes of visitors. The heart of the tropical rainforest in Kerala, in southern India, is a case in point. The Hotel Vaythhri consists of two tree houses built in the mid-1990s in the canopies of giant ficus trees. Traditionally, the people of Kerala built their homes high up in the branches, sometimes as high as two hundred feet (sixty meters) off the ground, as a way of avoiding predators and mosquitoes. From the vantage point of their huts, they could keep an eye on their crops and kill any marauding animals.

Down below, from the cottages built on solid ground, all that can be seen of the hotels are the platforms on which the rooms are built. To get to their room, visitors follow a winding path with a narrow bridge across a plunging precipice, or are swung up in a wicker basket as the counterweight—a water tank—fills up. The rooms are some ninety feet (twenty-eight meters) off the ground, on a solid branch which acts as a load-bearing wall. There are no interior walls; instead, visitors can roll down mats that are tied to the branches for privacy. The roof is made of palm leaves. Inside there is a wicker bed, an oil lamp, and a ficus branch growing out through an opening in the roof to provide some light. In the shower room, turmeric and red sandalwood powder take the place of soap, and rice husks are used instead of toothpaste. It is a place of utter peace. Absolute silence reigns during the day. The jungle comes alive at night, with a veritable symphony of mysterious, eerie animal cries. Bears and panthers growl nearby, while moths and flying squirrels, nearly as big as Yorkshire terriers, brush past. One visitor told us about her stay there: "I didn't sleep a wink all night! Like in an Orson Welles movie, my mind played tricks on me with every noise and every shadow cast by the oil lamp. It was like the monster you imagine under the bed when you are a child. You don't know where all these strange noises are coming from. That's probably the scariest thing: all you can do is guess! The most terrifying noises were the monkeys screaming. And during the night, my toothpaste and my shoes were nibbled by dormice. The best thing was definitely cleaning my teeth in the morning as the sun rose over the jungle."

Kenyan hunting lodges, Mongolian yurts, bungalows in Botswana, thatched huts on the Pacific atoll of Bora-Bora—all cater to Western tourists escaping for a few days and looking for a taste of adventure. A luxury floating hotel has recently opened on a turquoise lagoon in the Maldives. The rooms are a series of bungalows on piles—each with a terrace, pontoon, and jetty in New Zealand cedar, bamboo, and teak. They have all the creature comforts, but the hotel, in the end, is just a more sophisticated version of the Robinson Crusoe fantasy.

Hideaways have something to do with mobile, itinerant bodies, the bodies that we are, the house with the bodies that we have.

Gilles A. Tiberghien

GARDEN HIDEAWAYS

What would a garden be without a house? Houses anchor gardens in the world. Thanks to houses, gardens become places in their own right, inscribed in space, with an interior, an exterior—a complex universe. So there are places—a garden, a house—which shelter the thoughts of man, haunt his soul, give substance to his existence. They are his true refuge in the world, the only place where he can experience the feeling of being absolutely alive.

Un jardin pour soi, Catherine Laroze and Claire de Virieu

The little girl who plays in this hideaway in Fréjus, on the French Riviera, asked her grandmother to grow thorny plants around it so she would feel safe there.

The shed at the bottom of the garden. It has become a real cliché—the place where grandfather would spend his Sunday afternoons tinkering with his car. Until recently, sheds were hidden away behind a screen of bushes. Over the last few years, however, gardening enthusiasts and landscape architects have rediscovered the charms of these modest hideaways, and put them on proud display alongside their flowerbeds and vegetable patches. Sheds have made something of a comeback in public parks and garden festivals, too, where they are part of the show, just like architectural follies in the eighteenth century. Sheds are a symbol of man's attempts to tame nature.

The humble hideaway

The fashion for gardens with smooth lawns, gravel walks, and neatly trimmed trees—nature carefully under control—seems to be coming to an end. Gardeners are now more interested in making their patch of land an inviting, intimate place. Sheds are one of the key ingredients in this new, more relaxed style of garden. The return to a less formal, more spontaneous style, where charm takes precedence over neatness, reflects a need for nostalgia and tenderness. The new style of garden represents a lost Eden, a corner of paradise, far removed from the relentless pace of modern life. The humble shed has earned its place here, being both modest and useful. There are fashions for garden sheds, too; currently, the taste is for functional yet inventive styles.

The gardener and landscape architect Hugues Peuvergne has three sheds in his garden in Lagny-sur-Marne, near Paris. The first is made of wood. It has a double sloping roof and is covered in ivy, and is unremarkable in every way except for one feature which Peuvergne added as a joke: the door, which comes from a recently renovated café in the extremely chic Place des Vosges in Paris. He found the door in a dumpster, and likes to think it is enjoying its retirement away from the smoke and grime of Paris. His second hideaway is nestled in the branches of a gigantic thuja tree. His children love to play there, climbing on the huge branch that grows through the floor of the hut, and spying on their parents through the portholes that peep through the conifer's branches. The third hideaway is like a fairytale cottage, with its own little fence, vegetable patch, fountain, and even a mailbox.

Hugues Peuvergne believes there is no reason why even a humble tool-shed should be tucked away at the bottom of the garden. He prefers the idea that gardens are places to be lived in, and that sheds are a vital part of that. He explains: "It creates a presence. It gives the impression that the gardener has just stepped out, and that you can just sit and wait for a while for him to return." He sees garden hideaways as a way of bringing people closer to nature: "They allow me to connect people and plants."

Just ten years ago, Peuvergne's clients always asked him to hide their sheds behind a hedge. Now they spend as much time choosing a suitable site for the shed as they do on their flowered borders. Often, he is asked to build sheds that blend into the garden as if they have always been there. He says, "For ages, sheds were hidden away at the bottom of the garden. I want to do the exact opposite, and draw attention to them. Sheds can be as attractive as any other garden feature." He often drapes them with climbing plants, or places a gate, a bench, or a lantern by the door. He finds that sheds bring a new perspective to a narrow garden, hinting at hidden corners, and giving the illusion of more space. "For many years, gardens were all about esthetics, and were not meant to be lived in. I prefer to bring out their practical, useful side. People want to dig and plant in their gardens, not just sit and look at them. They want a place where they can go and be alone, rest, and meditate." Some of his clients have been Parisians who want a shed on their terrace or roof

The style of the hideaway must be in harmony with the atmosphere of the garden. It can be a serious, grown-up building on piles, as in the grounds of the Château de Gerfaut, in Azay-le-Rideau in the Loire valley (left), or a more modest, enchanting hut, as in the garden belonging to the landscape architect Hugues Peuvergne, in Lagny-sur-Marne, near Paris (facing page).

to have a place to go where the walls are not all smooth concrete. They like to feel the wooden planks under their fingers and have their own secret corner of nature in the heart of the city. It is an almost physical pleasure. These fragile, humble structures are an opportunity to rediscover the delights of creativity—of gardening, painting, sewing, writing. Peuvergne knows one family that commissioned a "nest" of wrought-iron overgrown with vegetation in the branches of an acacia, six and a half feet (two meters) off the ground.

Hugues Peuvergne has worked on an extraordinary variety of sheds made of reclaimed planks, oxidized metal, or with walls of curtains of creepers. A family from the chic Paris suburb of Neuilly commissioned a bold geometric design with narrow glass windows and walls of galvanized iron. All of Peuvergne's designs are inspired by the particular use the shed is destined for, in this case storing a moped. His final design was unique, in keeping with the style of the garden and the tastes of its owners. The garden was extremely narrow, and a traditional shed would simply have taken up too much space. The solution he came up with was at once elegant and simple. He placed the shed directly in front of the entrance to the garden, so that visitors have to walk around it to get a view of the house. This gives the home an air of coquettish mystery. From the house, the shed blocks the view of the gate, as if the garden were a world of its own, and the bustle of the street a distant dream.

For every one of his commissions, Peuvergne makes a particular point of meeting the whole family and listening to their ideas so that the final design is perfectly suited to their needs. The family in Neuilly were aficionados of contemporary art. Peuvergne was inspired by this to come up with a design characterized by bold, stark lines and materials. "Each shed has its own story to tell—they are the complete opposite of mass-produced lines," he says proudly. He likes to recount how one of his clients, a grandmother who commissioned a shed on stilts for her grandchildren, called him back several months after the work on the project had been completed. She had a new task for him: "The children want to spend Christmas in their hideaway. Could you come and fix it up with electricity?"

Hugues Peuvergne's sheds are not to be hidden away in the bushes: they are proudly on display. Unlike the mass-produced sheds on sale in garden centers, each design reflects something of the personality of the owner. It might be overgrown with flowers—the sign of a friendly welcome—or veiled in creepers, indicating a thoughtful, solitary disposition.

The author François Cavanna and the photographer Patricia Meaille noticed another trend for sheds during work on a book on gardens. Among other signs that people are once again glad to go out and get their hands dirty digging and planting, they noted, was the return of the outdoor toilet in a hut at the bottom of the garden! Cavanna writes with a wry smile of the "overwhelming beauty of these places, too long ignored by art lovers." It is true that there is often a hint of naive art about the garden shed, which is to architecture what graffiti is to art, or rap to poetry—an expression of popular culture.

The charm of the kitchen garden

The half-dilapidated shed, the skeletal hedge, and the tree, stripped of all its former glory—it is a miserable place. Is this the price to pay for freedom? Between the four walls of the shed, he can forget all the torments of the project; he feels protected. This is his universe. He built it with his own hands and decorated it himself. All around there is the garden, and on the other side of the gate, his neighbors. It's calm here.

Un jardin pour soi, Catherine Laroze and Claire de Virieu

For generations of men who worked in mines and factories their only recreation was a Sunday afternoon spent on their allotment. For charcoal-burners, resin-tappers, wine-producers, and jobbing-gardeners the shed itself was a place of work. Over the past few years, there has been growing interest in traditional kitchen gardens. Decorative cabbages are found on sale alongside rose bushes, and enthusiastic amateurs can learn about herbs and spices from specialist gardening programs. Of course, this is part of the current fashion for getting closer to nature, along with buying organic produce and recycling our waste. In our busy urban lives, where our streets are choked with pollution, and strawberries are on sale in December, it is a salutary lesson to watch vegetables and herbs growing at their own rate and to realize that there is nothing we can do to speed up the process. Gardening teaches us to nurture—even if it is just a tomato plant—and above all, to be patient.

The town of Chaumont-sur-Loire, south of Paris, is famous for its long-running garden festival. The 1999 festival was on the theme of the kitchen garden. The architects, landscape designers, artists, and gardeners took the theme to heart, coming up with some amazing creations. Jean-Luc Daneyrolles, a gardener based in the Lubéron mountains in the south of France, presented one of the most inventive designs. Entitled "A curious kitchen garden," it was based on a cross-shaped patch of land and included a gazebo in stripes of bright colors. As he says, "Kitchen gardens that produce food and sheds that store it are both part of the same primitive need. Gardens were the original form of agriculture, just as huts were the first houses. Both are blueprints or prototypes. Both are utopian ideals, connected to the notions of childhood, nature, and ecosystems. They are a nostalgic echo of a golden age, of dreams of childhood that we hang on to as they slip ever further away."

Another of the star gardens at the 1999 Chaumont festival set out to prove that kitchen gardens and sheds have a vibrant future. The landscape architects Patrick Nadeau and Vincent Dupont Rougier came up with a design for the garden of the future, calling it "The Nomad Garden." The design was basically a large box like a camping trailer which folds out into four sections: a stretch of latticework, a miniature greenhouse, a patch of furrowed soil for growing lettuce—and a space for resting in a deckchair. Vincent Dupont Rougier

The theme of the 1999 international garden festival held in Chaumont-sur-Loire, south of Paris, was the kitchen garden. Many of the gardens included a hut including the multi-colored gazebo in the "curious kitchen garden" designed by Jean-Luc Daneyrolles (left). Facing page: the third of the three huts planned by the modernist architects Jean-Marc Bourry and Marc Soucat. The vegetables are planted in containers watered by hanging watering cans.

This is a traditional allotment shed in the Ivry gardens, in the southern suburbs of Paris (facing page). Most of the allotments belong to retired couples, who can be seen there every day, winter and summer alike, taking a break at midday to eat the packed lunch they brought with them in a basket, as they did every day for forty years when they worked in the nearby factories.

The beloved old garden shed of our grandfathers has been brought up to date. This "nomad's garden" is an ultra-modern Utopia, designed by Patrick Nadeau and Vincent Dupont Rougier. The walls of their "garden-furniture" open up to reveal plants growing in pots or on lattices.

explains their inspiration: "We didn't want to fall into the nostalgia trap. We deliberately moved away from the image of the traditional garden shed, choosing instead a hi-tech design using the concept of technology transfer. We wanted to highlight the technology behind experimental greenhouse designs in an easily accessible manner."

However ephemeral they were designed to be, sheds have a habit of taking root. They settle down in gardens like a grandfather snoozing in an old armchair. This is particularly the case with allotments, the small patches of land used by working-class families for growing vegetables, which have often been in the same family for several generations. In Britain, allotments date back to the reign of Queen Elizabeth I, when the lands used by the commoners to graze their sheep were enclosed, and they were compensated with small plots of land. In the nineteenth century, allotments were seen as a way for factory workers of peasant stock to keep in touch with the land, provide food for their families, and keep them out of pubs and other dens of iniquity. The architect Edith-Claude Bouquin has written a history of allotments. "Sheds are an integral part of the allotment. They symbolize the ideal home in a corner of paradise—a modest dream, but one which is at least within reach." It must have been clear to many nineteenth-century factory workers that the shed on their patch of land was a far healthier place than their home, in the back streets. In this sense, the garden shed is emblematic of Rousseau's belief in the virtues of a primitive society in tune with nature.

After World War II, during which allotments played a vital part in the war effort as the major source of food all over Britain, kitchen gardens fell out of favor. It was not until the 1970s, the decade when environmental issues began to be of real concern, that allotments came back into fashion. The patches of land given over to allotments are often too small to be of interest to the building trade, or else in unsuitable locations, such as alongside railway lines or major roads. However small and straggling, allotments do provide welcome splashes

of green in what are often the poorest parts of cities. Allotments are a place where people can get away from the drudgery of their daily lives and work for their own pleasure.

We visited one allotment along an expressway in a working-class suburb south of Paris. The gardens and sheds have hardly changed for decades. They still have the same trellises and fold-away awnings as in vintage photographs dating from the early twentieth century. The only sign that times have changed is a sheet of corrugated iron here, a stretch of tarmac there. For generations, these sheds have been the only "vacation homes" local families could afford. The men would come out here every weekend to spend their few leisure hours playing cards or organizing *boules* contests, eating home-made sandwiches, and in more recent years, lighting up the barbecue. Over there, I spot an inflatable paddling pool between two rows of cabbages. Opposite, behind a neatly trimmed thuja hedge, I can just make out a pergola where a West Indian family plays host to dozens of friends almost every weekend. Some sheds have magnificent glass and wrought-iron doors that are far too grand for the surroundings—these belong to men who work on building sites and have been allowed to bring unwanted materials from demolition projects home with them. Each shed is different, and yet the allotments as a whole reflect the qualities of the community—thrift and good humor. They proudly show off the often extremely ingenious solutions they have found to specific problems—a veranda made of plastic sheeting, a pigeon loft cobbled together from leftover planks and a roll of chicken wire. The overall impression is, curiously, one of harmony.

This rather haphazard style of building does not meet with universal approval. Some local residents call it a shanty town and visual pollution and threaten to send in the bulldozers. The committee that runs the allotments has set out some ground rules: the sheds are to be no larger than forty-three square feet (four square meters), too small to fit a mattress (to discourage squatters), and each family is responsible for the upkeep of its patch of land. In another nearby suburb, the sheds were replaced by semicircular lockers. They were discreet, but the gardeners complained that they let in the rain. Of course, they were unhappy that the sheds they spent years building and improving had been replaced with new identical lockers. In 1988, the architect Renzo Piano, who came up with the revolutionary design for the Pompidou Center in Paris, was called in to look at the problem. He placed a curved awning over the locker, so that the rainwater trickled down into a barrel. He then rearranged them back to back in pairs, so that they looked like a bird spreading its wings. The rows of huts looked elegant, but proved rather impractical. Because the tools were stored horizontally, they dried out too slowly, and there was nowhere for the gardeners to change clothes. Some of the allotment holders have now put up a pergola or have grown a sheet of ivy on a trellis as an extension of the hut, creating their own changing-room.

Whatever the shortcomings of Renzo Piano's design, it did have the benefit of putting allotments and garden architecture firmly back in the spotlight. Other towns began to provide allotment sheds inspired by local traditions—egg-shaped steel huts for a steel-producing

Garden sheds come in many guises, from the rather grand version in the Parc de Saint-Cloud just west of Paris, to the lean-to made from reclaimed sheets of corrugated iron designed by Hugues Peuvergne (left), or the modest shed at the bottom of a family garden in Caen, Normandy, on the outskirts of a modern housing development (facing page).

region, for example—or, on the contrary, strikingly modern designs in concrete. For many people, it is a shame that allotment designs now tend to be architect-led rather than being the fruit of the skills and ingenuity of the people who use them. The researchers Jean-René Hissard and François Portet have written extensively on the subject. They are ardent advocates of this "popular, non-codified creativity," as they term this kind of organic, spontaneous architecture. They write, "Gardening and garden sheds, like Outsider Art, tend to bear witness to forms of creativity on the fringes of the dominant culture, and are indications of what men would be like if they were not conditioned by the cultural mandates they have subconsciously adopted." They introduce the concept of architecture without architects in communities where a professional architect's services would be financially beyond reach. Instead, other avenues are explored, for example reclaiming and recycling building materials and household trash, to create what the two researchers call "non-specialist architecture made for oneself and by oneself." Twenty-five years after Hissard and Portet first developed this concept, the sheds designed by architects for local councils for use in allotments are generally perfectly serviceable, but lacking in originality and imagination. Only the gardener can give them the personal touch.

Surprisingly, the allotment shed has proved a rich source of inspiration for professional landscape architects. The Copenhagen Architecture Park is located in an orchard twenty-five miles (forty kilometers) outside the Danish capital. Fourteen internationally-renowned architects were asked to come up with their own interpretation of traditional Danish allotments, the late nineteenth-century *Kolonihaven*. The challenge was to build a shed with a maximum surface area of sixty-five square feet (six square meters). Freed from the technical constraints of larger buildings, the architects let their imaginations run wild. The Swiss designer Mario Botta came up with a plan for a miniature wooden fortress with two enclosed staircases leading to a roof terrace. The only light comes from small holes, making it possible, as Botta writes, "to recapture the feeling of being a child hiding in a box and looking out at the world through little holes." The roof terrace is lined with a "hedge" of bamboo pales. The Swedish architect Ralph Erskine was also inspired by childhood hideaways. His design was a tall tower that played with the notions of interior and exterior. He describes it as "a small tower to satisfy our childish pleasure of climbing trees, or our adult joy in getting to the top, floating above the park in the middle of the leafy canopy. Having arrived at the top you can hoist up your basket of bread, fruit, cheese and wine and rest around the table with good friends, birds and butterflies. In a large box in the middle a small flowering tree grows up through the table." The French architect Dominique Perrault enclosed a tree in a glass shell, like a treasure. "This shell of glass captures nature that man both owns and protects."

These designs, although inspired by Danish workers' allotments, are in fact closer in inspiration to nineteenth-century architectural follies—whimsical, outlandish, sometimes downright bizarre. As Hissard and Portet point out, sheds are on the fringes of mainstream architecture, like follies, and are therefore marginal and eccentric almost by definition.

Modern follies

"Have you seen my wife?" Eduard asked, making ready to leave. "Over in the new grounds," the Gardener replied. "It is today she finishes the little summer-house she has been building by the rocks facing the Hall. Everything has turned out beautifully. Your Lordship will be sure to like it. The views are excellent: the village down below, the church a little to the right—you look out almost directly over the steeple—the Hall and the gardens opposite."

The Elective Affinities, Johann Wolfgang von Goethe, tr. David Constantine

FOLLY: A folly is often thought of as an extravagant structure built as a conversation piece or a sculptural element in the landscape, typically without any functional purpose.

Quote from www.loggia.com, online architecture dictionary

The humble garden shed might at first glance seem to be at the opposite end of the scale to the eighteenth-century follies that were built by landowners eager to flaunt their wealth. Follies were designed to provide pleasant places to rest, picturesque views, and a place to shelter in case of rain on the grounds of the great stately homes. They often imitated particular styles of architecture—classical Greek temples or Turkish mosques. Today, however, garden hideaways are increasingly taking on a decorative role, and the whimsical designs of specialist architects like Hugues Peuvergne often play with architectural conventions or even ignore them altogether, bringing them close to follies.

The *Jardins de la Brande* lie nestled in the heart of the rolling hills of the Dordogne, in southwestern France. In the center of the gardens is a magnificent hideaway of chestnut wood, some four feet (one hundred and twenty centimeters) in diameter. Visitors crawl in through a round door set near the ground. Once inside, it is very dark, as if you were standing in the bottom of a well; the only light filters down from the open top. It is also pleasantly cool, especially on the swelteringly hot summer days that are a local specialty. The perfect children's hideaway was created in 2000 by Cyril Delage and Virginie Écorce for an exhibition organized by a local nurseryman, Philippe Burey, who loves hideaways in all shapes and forms. The designers harvested the wood for the hideaway from local trees. The walls are covered with a layer of adobe from a nearby clay pit. Delage and Écorce believe that hideaways should be built using natural and recycled materials wherever possible, calling on local crafts, in keeping with the spirit of adventure they embody.

The hideaway in the Jardins de la Brande proved popular, and the couple's newly founded company, the Atelier Virginie Écorce, was flooded with orders. As Delage says, "It's one of the failings of our contemporary society that we call people in to do things rather than

Nicole Cottarel's tree house (facing page) is a rope net slung between the branches of a chestnut tree in the Jardins de la Brande, in the Dordogne. The walls are barely there, but once inside, the structure feels very protective. It is strangely reminiscent of the Gardener's Huts, a series of engravings by François Houtin (left).

getting on and doing the job ourselves. I suppose it's like people commissioning follies in centuries past." Many orders are placed by Parisians wanting an unusual shed for their vacation home, and as a result, they stand unused for most of the year. "Our clients are happy to own one of our hideaways, but they don't want to live in it. They're just garden decorations, and maybe what we like to call mental decorations—they store them in a little corner of their mind and get pleasure from simply imagining the time they could be spending there."

Delage and Écorce draw attention to another thorny question. "You can't commission a hideaway, or build one for someone else. Although we spend a lot of time talking the

Follies first appeared in English gardens in the eighteenth century as places to stop while strolling around the garden and enjoy the view. There are a great number of follies in Holland, particularly in gardens by canals. They look like delightful places to stop for a cup of tea. Virginie Écorce has created a small folly (right) using chestnut wood.

design over with our clients, the structure will always have a certain degree of spontaneity, as the final result depends very much on the sorts of building materials we find locally." There is no way of planning ahead that a branch will be strong enough to bear the weight of a tree house. Such unforeseen details are precisely what makes each hideaway unique, and what makes each project so endlessly fascinating for Écorce and Delage. For example, one particular client had a two-hundred-year-old thuja tree in the garden. The two designers came up with a plan for a hideaway tucked away between the branches that sweep down to the ground where they propagate underground runners before reaching skywards again. Through the leaves, you can just see the shelter built around the trunk. Delage says, "Hideaways are undisciplined architecture. They are built using modern, industrial materials found locally and recycled, without fussing about what the materials were initially designed to do or paying heed to current architectural thinking."

The desire to create a whimsical garden decorated with eccentric, anachronistic buildings is not modern. In fact, it even predates the eighteenth-century craze for follies. As early as the Renaissance, gardens were seen as places of enchantment and recreation. The garden of Bomarzo in Italy is a fine example. It was commissioned by one of the Orsini princes, and designed by Pirro Ligorio. The grounds are full of odd statues and other bizarre, even eerie features, including a cave said to lead straight to Hell. The rock face around the cave has been carved to resemble a giant's face, and visitors enter the cave through his gaping maw.

Follies first came into fashion in eighteenth-century England. The craze soon reached the continent. Wealthy landowners paid the best-known gardeners of the day—men like Capability Brown and Humphry Repton—to plan their grounds and choose the best site for a ruined Greek temple. Tree houses were particularly popular, as were miniature chalets in the Alpine style and other more exotic designs such as Chinese tea pavilions. Some went so far as to hire hermits to live in their hermitages, for that added touch of authenticity! The philosopher Jean-Jacques Rousseau's vision of the benefits of a pure, simple, rural life was highly influential. He inspired Marie Antoinette to keep a flock of sheep to play with in the Petit Trianon, a grand folly in the grounds of the palace of Versailles. In Johann Wolfgang von Goethe's novel *The Elective Affinities*, published in 1809, the aristocratic heroine, Charlotte, spends all her time in the garden, bending nature to her will, creating a fashionable English-style garden: "When the volumes were opened they saw for each case an outline of the terrain and drawings of the landscape in its first rough and natural state, then on other pages depictions of the changes wrought on it by art in such a way as to utilize and enhance all the good already present there. The transition to their own property, to their own surroundings and to what might be made of them, was an easy one . . . they devised an easier ascent to the ridge; and they would put up a sort of pavilion high on the slopes against a pleasant little copse; it would bear on the Hall, it would be visible from the Hall windows, and from it the Hall and gardens would be overlooked." One of Charlotte's earliest projects, described in the first pages of the novel, is a moss-covered summerhouse, where she invites her guests like a little girl playing at holding a tea party.

Of course, there are many differences between the eighteenth-century fashion for follies and the current vogue for garden hideaways, but there are nonetheless some interesting points of comparison: both are fanciful variations on traditional rustic architecture and both imply a deep need to reconnect with our environment and to experience the peace that comes from contemplating the natural world. However, it is true to say that in the eighteenth century, follies were commissioned by aristocrats eager to flaunt their wealth and taste, whereas today's garden hideaways are a more private pleasure. By and large, people do not order a hideaway as a way of showing off to the neighbors, but as a way of proving to themselves that they are still capable of appreciating the simple things in life.

The landscape architect Antoine Arnoux, the man behind the *Jardins de la Licorne* in Normandy, likes to compare hideaways to stage scenery or costumes. Many of his clients commission hideaways for their vacation homes in the seaside resort of Deauville or for their manors nestled in the lush green valleys inland. He described a typical commission for us. A Swiss businessman wanted a gray-and-white playhouse for his children. Arnoux designed an intimate, magical space that seemed to be set in another dimension: a tiny walled garden with four doors labeled Hearts, Diamonds, Clubs, and Spades. The hideaway was sheltered by two tall trees specially chosen for their unusual foliage: one with leaves in the form of butterfly wings, the other's leaves resembling crumpled handkerchiefs. The hut has a terrace of blue pebbles, shutters, and a canopy over the door—a real fairytale cottage.

Many of Arnoux's clients commission "fake" sheds that will never be used, just to create a rustic atmosphere, even using props like watering-cans and rakes to complete the image. They refuse to let him use plastic, which is too modern and would look out of place in their rural idyll. As Antoine says, "There is definitely an aspect of the theater set about these hideaways. Often, I find that my pretty, idyllic hut is meant to hide the real tool shed, which was designed to be purely functional rather than esthetically pleasing." He continues, "Just like in a film, the gardener has to think about tracking shots, and imagine the camera panning round from one scene to another." Whether he gives them a dramatic starring role as a central feature of the garden or a more modest supporting role alongside a fabulous rose garden or lily pond, his sheds always steal the limelight. Over the years, Arnoux has noted that the site chosen for the shed really does make a difference. On top of a hill, for instance, it will look ethereal and distant, whereas a shed tucked away in a clump of bushes will look mysterious, even ominous. He has also noticed that sheds are a seasonal phenomenon. They seem to go into hibernation over the winter, while their owners remain

Follies, temples, and topiary designs—for his Garden Sheds series, François Houtin produced twelve engravings of intertwining branches and faintly sinister plants forming eerie fairytale shelters (top right and bottom left). In a similar style is the hut made of chestnut stakes (top left). It was designed by the gardener Philippe Stoffaes, who was directly inspired by François Houtin's art. A circular shelter nestled between two tree trunks—made of concrete. Fabien Rochoux presented this giant squirrel's nest at an art exhibition on the theme of trees and shrubs at the Parc Floral in Paris (bottom right). It was made using the old-fashioned rocaille technique.

François Houtin has built a hideaway based on his own engravings. He came up with the design for the garden festival held in the Parc de Saint-Cloud, using hornbeam, twisted willow, and climbing ivy. The design symbolizes the ill-famed tavern in Gounod's opera Faust *(facing page). Light pours into the hideaway from the open ceiling (right).*

snug and warm indoors, and to come back to life with the garden in spring. This is why Antoine Arnoux finds his work so fascinating.

Gardens have always been used to theatrical effect. The art of rocaille, invented in seventeenth-century Italy but now almost lost, is a superb example of art imitating life. Rocaille workers work with stone—nowadays concrete—which they sculpt to resemble organic materials such as wood or shells. Fabien Rochoux has devoted his life to learning and promoting the ancient technique, carving branches out of blocks of cement, down to the very last detail. He has a workshop near Creil, north of Paris. His sheds are most unusual, and have proved rather too avant-garde for the French market which associates the art of rocaille with early-twentieth-century kitsch. While waiting for the market to develop, Rochoux has not been wasting his time: he has filled entire sketchpads with drawings of imaginary huts, sheds, and kiosks in cement. In 1998, he was commissioned to build four rocaille shelters in the Parc Floral de Vincennes, just outside Paris. He came up with intriguing designs: a Cinderella pumpkin, a Robinson Crusoe hut, a dome of branches propped on two concrete tree trunks, and a squirrel's nest. This last design, which he describes as "A bit naive, like something out of a cartoon," weighs a ton and a half, and measures eleven feet (three and a half meters) in height. The concrete leaves are painted green. The walls are decorated with concrete branches.

The designs have been criticized by people who say concrete is too urban a material for rustic hideaways. Rochoux disagrees. He believes rocaille is perfect for shelters: "It answers the same deep-rooted need as the hideaway itself—the need to create a private world, to feel protected. Rocaille can conjure up the atmosphere of a romantic park, a dark forest, or a country garden. It brings the spirit of the forest into the garden and gives it a soul." Rocaille constructions have a way of blending into their natural surroundings. Although they are made of a man-made material, they age naturally. Emerald-green moss and blue-gray lichen grow on the walls and roof. As Rochoux says, "A rocaille building overgrown with vegetation resembles the ruins of an ancient civilization. Even if I built the 'ruins' myself, and I know that they don't have roots and are just a stage set, I find myself being taken in by the illusion." Rochoux loves working with concrete. He can twist his concrete branches around his buildings in ways that would be impossible with real trees. He continues, "My rocaille shelters look like something out of a fairy tale because they go wherever my imagination takes them. I want to give gardens such a striking presence that visitors half expect to see a mythical creature or a fantastic genie."

The new follies commissioned for parks and gardens herald a new relationship between nature and the built environment. Exhibitors at the Chaumont-sur-Loire garden festival have shown designs inspired by the relative impermanence of sheds and hideaways, tending towards ever more adaptable gardens. The architects Edouard François and Duncan Lewis invented the "soft greenhouse," a flexible cube of transparent plastic with a bamboo frame. Two other exhibitors, the biologist Patrick Blanc and the engineer Gilles Ebersolt, designed a pergola made of Kevlar nets strung on poles. Kevlar is principally used in the aerospace industry and Formula One racing. Blanc and Ebersolt came to work together when the biologist was looking for a new design for a laboratory for use in the field. Blanc specializes in jungle environments, and needed a hut that could be slung in the branches in the rainforest canopy, several dozen feet off the ground.

Facing page: basket maker Eric Renault's living willow hut grows and flourishes with the seasons. Using traditional basket-weaving techniques, he wove the dry willow branches and living branches together in the Jardins de la Brande, in the Perigord region of France. It is in the same spirit as an engraving from the Garden Sheds series by François Houtin (left).

Architects no longer feel that hideaways are beneath them. Like the great landscape architects of the eighteenth century, they are rediscovering the delights of playing with purely decorative constructions. However, unlike their illustrious predecessors, they tend to work in harmony with the landscape rather than altering the lay of the land in keeping with their vision. Phyllis Richardson, author of a book on the subject of small-scale architectural projects, believes that constructions designed to celebrate the natural world can come in a whole range of different forms, from underground bunkers, or blinds on stilts offering a panoramic view of the landscape, to the type of huts that our ancestors might have built thousands of years ago. She writes that satisfying the need to spend time alone serves a number of purposes: allowing people to watch the world go by and to contemplate their own existence, to seek the tranquillity needed to recharge their batteries, and to find inspiration.

Architects have always built their own dream hideaways to escape from the pressures of the office. Hans-Peter Wörndl designed and built a hideaway, all in wood, on the shores of the Mondsee in Austria. He christened the extremely modern design GucklHupf. It was an observation post which played on the theme of opening and shutting, with a system of sliding wooden panels. The numerous windows offered panoramic views over the lake and the surrounding countryside, so that the owner could contemplate the way the quality of light changed as the day progressed. Sadly, GucklHupf is no longer standing.

Other well-known architects have also built hideaways that are more like sculptures than homes. Sir Norman Foster built a "cockpit" overlooking a Cornish estuary, and Thomas Heatherwick designed a belvedere for his estate in Belzay, Northumberland, that, from a distance, looked just like a sea urchin. The London-based agency Softroom opted for a futuristic design for a building overlooking Kielder Water in the Northumbrian forest. The building looks as if it could have almost been dropped by a spaceship. Inside, the steel walls are coated with a thin layer of gold powder. Visitors can sit inside looking out over the lake.

These last two designs are certainly striking, but, in their own way, they pay homage to nature. They are places of contemplation and reflection. Like the eighteenth-century follies, they reflect man's preoccupation with questions about his relationship with the natural world.

Reliving Robinson's Adventures

Where am I to sleep
And what am I to eat,
I shall famish and starve on the island!
I haven't much society,
There isn't much variety,
I've nothing for my dinner
And ditto for my tea.
I have no bed to lie upon,
No line my clothes to dry upon,
In fact I may say candidly that I am up a tree!

"The Adventures of Robinson Crusoe," Howard Clifton's Latest Songs

In the mid-nineteenth century, a wealthy French businessman by the name of Gueusquin read Daniel Defoe's great novel *The Life and Strange Surprising Adventures of Robinson Crusoe, of York, Mariner*, first published in 1719. This gave him an idea for a new business giving Parisians a taste of the lifestyle Robinson led on his island. He decided to build a restaurant in the branches of a group of venerable old chestnut trees in a suburb of Paris, Le Plessis-Piquet, which was renamed Le Plessis-Robinson in 1905, in honor of the restaurant. He built spiral staircases around the trunks, put in flooring, romantic bowers, and thatched roofs, and tucked tables discreetly among the branches. The provisions were winched up in baskets, much to the delight of the diners.

The restaurant was an immediate success. The earliest clients were well-heeled gentlemen in tailcoats and ladies in extravagant hats. Isabella of Spain and Victor Hugo were said to be guests. Before long, Gueusquin's restaurant had a reputation as a place for romantic rendezvous, doubtless because the couples could hide discreetly behind the branches.

A number of other entrepreneurs seized on the idea and opened rival restaurants—the Grand Saint-Eloi, the Arbre de la Terrasse, the Escargot Doré, the Gros Châtaignier, to name a few. The fashion for treetop dining reached its heyday between 1900 and 1914. It is doubtless that part of the reason for its popularity was the freedom it offered in a society bound at that time by stifling etiquette. Perched up in a tree, no one will worry if you use the wrong knife to eat your fish!

This sense of playful irreverence was recreated at the 2000 Chaumont-sur-Loire garden festival, in France, in Hugues Peuvergne's Straw Gardens. The design featured a pile of bales of hay topped with a hideaway of interwoven branches. To see this inaccessible refuge up close from belvederes some seven feet (two meters) off the ground,

This treetop restaurant served meals in Le Plessis-Robinson, near Paris, in 1908 (facing page). The meals were hoisted into the tree in large baskets using a rope and pulley system. The engraving on the left show a treetop restaurant dating from 1880.

The landscape architect Hugues Peuvergne came up with a design for a straw hut using piles of bales topped with a hideaway of plaited straw. The design towered over the Chaumont-sur-Loire garden festival (facing page). Right: A drawing of a hideaway inspired by Robinson Crusoe's parasol, printed in 1848 by Victor Petit in a collection entitled Country Habitations, *including houses, villas, chalets, pavilions, kiosks, parks, and gardens.*

visitors had to find a hidden door and negotiate their way through a maze made of walls of hay bales. Only then could they admire the surrounding landscape from this extraordinary perspective. Peuvergne is well aware of the potential for transgression of the hideaways he builds. He laughed aloud as he told us how he caught the owner of one newly finished hideaway hiding in it from his wife so that he could sneak a cigarette. Another took his wife and children down to sleep in the hut at the bottom of the garden, so that he could scare the children by telling them ghost stories.

The notion of transgression certainly has an erotic component, explored by D. H. Lawrence in his masterful novel *Lady Chatterley's Lover*. Lady Chatterley cannot experience physical pleasure in the great hall where she lives with her impotent husband. She discovers the joys of lovemaking in a tumbledown cottage in the woods. "She saw a secret little clearing, and a secret little hut made of rustic poles [...] The keeper in his shirt-sleeves was kneeling, hammering. [...] "I wondered what the hammering was," she said, feeling weak and breathless, and a little afraid of him, as he looked so straight at her.[...] "Come and sit' 'ere i' th' 'ut," he said [...] She obeyed him. [...] It was a jumble, but also it was a sort of sanctuary. [...] So she sat in the doorway of the hut in a dream, utterly unaware of time and of particular circumstances. She was so drifted away that he glanced up at her quickly, and saw the utterly still, waiting look on her face. To him it was the look of waiting. And a little thin tongue of fire suddenly flickered in his loins, at the root of his back, and he groaned in spirit."

Gardens were often places of erotic adventure in the eighteenth century. The paintings of Jean-Antoine Watteau are full of libertines flirting in leafy bowers. There is something undeniably sexual about the earthy, musky scent that often hangs in the air of garden sheds. It is as if a building set in the heart of nature invited erotic play as a way of stepping outside the normal social conventions. There is also the temptation to succumb to voyeurism, to creep up to the worm-eaten old shed at the bottom of the garden and peer in the dusty windows. . .

In Goethe's *Elective Affinities*, Charlotte's summerhouse is a setting where the unresolved erotic tension that eventually destroys the couple is to the fore. "Charlotte was at the door to welcome her husband. He sat where she placed him so that through windows and door he could oversee at a glance the different views . . . He was pleased, and expressed the hope that spring would soon bring to everything a yet more abundant life. 'My only criticism,' he added, 'would be that one is perhaps a little cramped here.' 'Room enough for the two of us,' Charlotte replied. 'There is indeed,' said Eduard, 'and

for a third, no doubt.' 'Why not?' Charlotte replied, 'and even for a fourth.'" The couple invite their friends, Ottilie and the Captain, to visit them in the summerhouse. The stage is set for the unleashing of the adulterous passions that are the novel's major theme. Later in the novel Charlotte, sorely tried, seeks solitary solace in her summerhouse: "Bowing hastily she turned away and hurried down to the summer-house. Long before she got there the tears had started from her eyes, and she flung herself into the narrow confines of that little hermitage and gave herself over entirely to a grief, a passion, a despair of whose possibility only a moment since she had had not the slightest apprehension."

Such erotic scenes set in hideaways, huts, sheds, and outbuildings are extremely common in literature. The 2002 Chaumont-sur-Loire garden festival was on the theme of eroticism in the garden. The architects Christophe Ponceau and Bertrand Houin designed a "playful labyrinth and screen for voyeurs," which contained cone-shaped wicker huts "for solitary pleasures and unforeseen encounters." Charline Pipard, Anne Levillain, and Pierre Gragnic designed an "interlacing garden" featuring a pergola shaped like a red-and-black corset, overgrown with climbing plants like caressing fingers. Then there was Tom Thumb's Garden Party, a project by fine arts students working in collaboration with Pierre-Alexandre Collin, which led the visitor through a field of hemp, past a garden planted with ginger and ginseng, and on to a mysterious construction scattered with keyholes for visitors to peek through.

Left shows a rustic belvedere from the collection of one hundred drawings printed in 1848 by Victor Petit. The famous chapel in Allouville-Bellefosse, in Normandy (facing page), is in the trunk of an oak tree thirteen centuries old. The trunk in fact contains two chapels, one built above the other. The earlier of the two, Our Lady of Peace, was built into the hollow trunk as early as the seventeenth century.

Nature and Culture

It seems to me that hideaways are places where art and nature meet: they reconnect us with the origins of art and civilization and conjure up the development of humanity as a whole, as well as our development as individuals.

Nature, Art, Paysage, Gilles A. Tiberghien

Garden hideaways must be in harmony with the land around them, like this phantasmagoric "ghost train" in the Jardins de la Licorne, in Normandy (facing page). The landscape architect Antoine Arnoux set up the basic structure in Moroccan ironwork, and the roof, which he sees as a protective symbol and essential element. The huts themselves are just one part of the garden's grand design. Arnoux also designed this half-timbered shelter (right) for a site in Normandy. He believes that his shelters are alive: as he says, "they remain discreet, are sometimes reborn, and become ever more dilapidated over the generations, over the lifetimes of their owners."

Gardens are where man explores his potential to dominate nature and shape it to his own will, creating a new balance of power between man and the natural environment, which for millennia forged our common destiny. The garden hideaways we have seen are a point of connection between nature and culture—they represent at once a civilized space and an extension of the local environment, built using recycled natural materials. They are modern follies, bold displays of cultural and architectural extravagance. But there is also something earthy and instinctive about them. As the ecologist Bernard Brun writes, "Their ambiguity comes from the fact that on the one hand they are constructed, produced, named, and vested with a symbolic role, making them a cultural product in their own right, while on the other hand, they are built in harmony with nature—'real' nature, which provides the raw materials for the construction but which is also a source of danger, and then 'imaginary' nature, which can be compared to the childhood wishes and desires that adolescents have to leave behind as they enter adulthood."

For eighteenth-century thinkers, the fashion for garden follies was an exploration of the dialectic between nature and culture, a vital question for the Age of Enlightenment, which looked to the origins of humanity for answers about their own society. Their follies, like our garden hideaways, were the architectural component of their philosophy of man's relation to nature. From there to investigating the origins of architecture itself is but a short step.

MODERN HIDEAWAYS

I have a castle on the Riviera, measuring 3.66 by 3.66 meters. It's for my wife; it's extravagantly comfortable and generous.

Le Corbusier

This red cube, built of bricks and wood, was designed by the artist Gloria Friedmann and the architect Adelfo Scaranello. It does not have running water or electricity. It looks as if it just mysteriously materialized one day on the edge of a pond in the Haute-Marne region of France.

Hideaways let our imaginations take flight. Mobile and ephemeral, they symbolize the free, nomadic spirit. Built in the heart of nature, often using recycled materials, they reflect modern concerns about protecting the environment. They follow the personal development of their owners, who add a window here or knock down a wall there, as their tastes change. Hideaways are the most intimate form of architecture.

Many forward-thinking and innovative architects are today turning to hideaways for inspiration, precisely because of these qualities. While the trend in recent years has been for ever more monumental and impersonal designs, leading exponents of modernism are experimenting with micro-architecture, revolutionary designs that are half-shed, half-furniture, giving people new ways of interacting with their home. And while technology has long been seen as a panacea for every ill, it is becoming ever more apparent that the solution to some design problems lies not in ever greater complexity, but in minimalist simplicity.

Professional architecture journals have recently begun to pay attention to the phenomenon of micro-architecture in general and

113

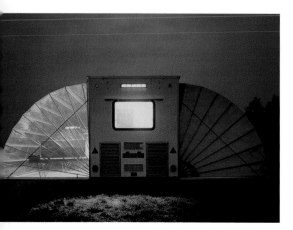

Édouard Böthlink's Markies is a cross between a caravan and a fisherman's hut. The walls can be folded up and down with a motor. Part of the terrace, sheltered by a transparent windbreak, opens towards the shore. At the other end of the hut, part of which can be folded away, the bedroom resembles a snail shell. The permanent structure at the center of the building houses the kitchen and toilet.

to hideaways in particular. In 2002, the Villa Noailles, an arts center in Hyères on the French Riviera, invited selected designers to design a "life module" in which it would be possible to work, rest, have friends around, and sleep, in a space no larger than 215 square feet (20 square meters). The two designers from the Delo Lindo agency came up with a light wooden structure with numerous apertures. The Radi Agency invented a simple yet ingenious cottage with walls that folded out to increase the surface area. The brothers Erwan and Ronan Bouroullec designed a house made of sheets of polystyrene that could be slotted into metal struts to create a space of precisely the desired size and shape. The structure was light and easy to put up and take down—an ultra-contemporary hideaway.

In architectural terms, hideaways are icons of simplicity and imagination. They are a source of inspiration for countless designers looking for a way to move beyond technical constraints, strict planning laws, and conventional architectural canons, and reconnect with the sense of breaking boundaries and the sheer fun of playing with materials that hooked them on design in the first place. Because they are, by definition, small-scale structures, hideaways are perfect for trying out new ideas that can be as extravagant or as whimsical as the designer's imagination can make them. Ecological, mobile, and adaptable—these designs are showing the way for the homes of the future.

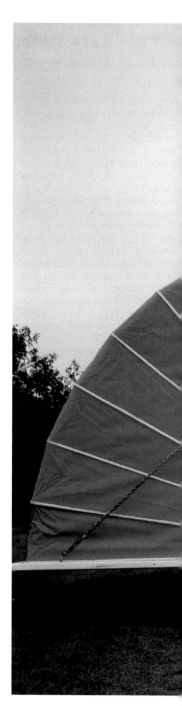

The myth of primitive hideaways

Therefore it was the discovery of fire that originally gave rise to the coming together of men, to the deliberative assembly, and to social intercourse. And so, as they kept coming together in greater numbers into one place . . . and being able to do with ease whatever they chose with their hands and fingers, they began in that first assembly to construct shelters.

De Architectura, Book 2, Chapter 1, Vitruvius, tr. Morris Hicky Morgan

Joep Van Lieshout chose to develop an ideally nomadic, flexible design in line with what he believes to be the future of architecture. He used a new polyester resin to mold his "mobile life units" as a single piece (facing page). Inside the cabin, the shelves, table, bed, and washroom facilities are all part of the same mold as the walls. Right: the fisherman's hut, another creation from Joep Van Lieshout's studio.

Vitruvius, Abbot Laugier, Quatremère de Quincy—all the great architectural theorists have traced the history of architecture back to primitive huts. In terms of architectural history, hideaways have become a fundamental concept, an inspirational icon at the heart of every new design principle. A founding myth that can give rise to the most classical or the most radical interpretations. Every generation has rediscovered the fundamental role of the primitive hut described by Joseph Rykwert in his book *On Adam's House in Paradise: The Idea of the Primitive Hut in Architectural History.*

Vitruvius, who lived in the first century B.C.E., wrote about the mystical power of huts in *De Architectura*: "Some made them of green boughs, others dug caves on mountain sides, and some, in imitation of the nests of swallows and the way they built, made places of refuge out of mud and twigs. Next, by observing the shelters of others and adding new details to their own inceptions, they constructed better kinds of huts as time went on."

Vitruvius was rediscovered in the eighteenth century, an age of great explorations. The French explorer Lafitau studied Native American habitations, and theorists began examining the history of architecture as a way of understanding their own world. The historian and philosopher Abbot Laugier imagined an ideal form of primitive hut that our earliest ancestors built to protect themselves from the elements:

Man wanted to build a dwelling that would protect him without burying him. A few branches cut down in the forest were the materials he needs for his plan. He chose four of the strongest, which he raised perpendicular to the ground and arranged in a square. Above, he placed four others diagonally, and on top of these he fixed others at a slant so that they formed a point. He covered this sort of roof with leaves so that neither sun nor rain could get through, and there was his home. . . . The little rustic hut that I have just described is the model on which all the magnificent designs in the history of architecture are based. Only by recreating the simplicity of this first model can we avoid basic mistakes and attain veritable perfection.

Abbot Laugier based his theory of neoclassical architecture on this myth of the first hut.

Le Corbusier's Cabin

Space and light and order. Those are the things that men need just as much as they need bread or a place to sleep.

Le Corbusier

*The architect
Le Corbusier spent
two months every
summer in his seaside
cottage overlooking
the bay in Roquebrune-
Cap-Martin on the
French Riviera. He
used to say he felt so at
ease that he would like
to end his days there.
His wish was granted;
he died while bathing
in the bay in 1965.*

Every revolution in architectural design stakes its claim to be a radical new departure on its reinterpretation of the most basic element in architecture—the hut. Le Corbusier, one of the most visionary of twentieth-century architects, drew on the hut as a source of inspiration, seeing it as the essence of good architecture—an archetypal geometric design on a human scale. "The path is as straight as his tools, his efforts, and the era allow. The poles of the tent form a square, a hexagon, or an octagon. The palisade forms a rectangle with four right angles. The door of the hut opens in line with the gate in the fence." Le Corbusier saw that huts had valuable lessons to offer in terms of simplicity and economy, and a more direct relationship between man and his environment.

Huts were more than just a concept for Le Corbusier. In 1952, he built his own one hundred and seventy-square-feet (sixteen-square-meter) hideaway in Roquebrune-Cap-Martin, on the French Riviera. The apparent simplicity of the hideaway belied its architectural complexity. The minimalist shelter of pine bark was perfectly adapted to the site. It was shaped like a swastika, a symbol of life in India, where Le Corbusier had spent two months traveling earlier that year. Outside, in the garden overlooking the Mediterranean, he had a small shower room and studio in the sort of workman's hut found on building sites.

*Le Corbusier developed
an innovative theory
of the minimal
dwelling space, inspired
by his research into
Oriental and Indian
architecture. He put
it into practice by
designing a complex
architectural ensemble,
with separate zones
for night and day,
for people living in
very small spaces.*

Ecological Hideaways

Topographies, the direction of the wind and the rain—all this cosmic data is inscribed in this architecture. Huts like this are an extension of geography. What is particular about huts is that the gap between their inhabitants and the environment is reduced. Huts are witnesses to human genius, their capacity to develop a culture, to speak the idea they have of themselves and their place in the order of creation, and at the same time, to interpret their environment, their relationship with their surroundings, with the earth, with geography.

La Cabane, figure géopoétique de l'architecture, Jean-Paul Loubes

The Red Cube (facing page), designed by Gloria Friedmann, is in an isolated valley in the Haute-Marne region, east of Paris. It invites visitors to re-engage with nature. Right: Jean-Philippe Vassal and Jeanne Lacaton set out to adapt the traditional architecture of the fishing huts in the Bassin d'Arcachon. They came up with a galvanized steel hut on piles, with trees growing through it. It can be rented by the day or the week.

Hideaways do not clash with the environment; they blend into their surroundings. This contrasts with the massive concrete blocks that have for the last few decades blighted our landscapes, insensitive to the environment. Hideaways tend to use recycled or reclaimed materials, and thus reflect a much more environmentally friendly approach to the construction process.

Many architects have been directly inspired by the simplicity of primitive huts and nomadic tents. James Wines' book *Green Architecture* is a case in point. It showcases small constructions built in harmony with nature, some of which use recycled materials in unusual and innovative ways. In 1993, the Swiss architect Peter Vetsch "buried" nine houses under a layer of turf, like grottoes tucked into folds in the earth. The British architect David Lea came up with a design which he christened the Studio in the West Country, a contemporary cottage with large bay windows, built using natural materials where possible and with minimal use of modern technology. The roof is thatched, the cement walls are mixed with horse hair for strength and are insulated with straw, and the frame is formed of wooden arches. The French designer Jean-Philippe Vassal was inspired by traditional building techniques he studied in Niger to develop a method of putting up light structures "almost intuitively, looking around to find whatever materials are lying around." His Maison Latapie on the shores of the lac d'Arcachon in southwestern France was built round the pine trees and sand dunes. The house is raised on piles. Six pine trees grow through the building.

Édouard François says that, "Our society is witnessing the end of an architectural era—the age of modernity and Le Corbusier. Now it is up to us to create a new era." He has created a building in Montpellier, on France's Mediterranean coast, which literally grows. The walls are formed of rocks planted with seeds in the crevices, held in place by a wire net. He believes that hideaways could be a metaphor for a new architectural era, one that places a premium on harmony between the interior and exterior of a building. He continues, "Modernity is about hygiene and abstraction. Hideaways are the complete opposite: they are about the night, trees, the jungle canopy, the cries of screech owls, fungi. Studying hideaways is a great way to step back from the modern world and to come up with truly innovative designs." He has his own family hideaway on the banks of the Seine, in Fontainebleau, south of Paris. He calls it his "picnic chest." It is just a rough, simple hut, set in a leafy grove. When he was invited to contribute a design to the Saint Cloud Garden Festival, he came up with a leather hideaway. He placed it in the branches of a tree, where it could only be reached by a narrow staircase. "I began thinking about hideaways about fifteen years ago. Hideaways mean pleasure, and I want to bring a sense of fun back into architecture, which has become far too serious today." Every apartment in his green building in Montpellier has a wooden balcony that can only be reached by a narrow walkway. He likes to compare the design to a fortress whose inhabitants have decided to finish the construction themselves, just like in medieval villages.

Mobility and separation

A rich vein awaits exploration: simple, rural habitations, that could be farms, or castles, or cabins. . . . Their language is not grand rhetoric, but skill. We must seek inspiration in their tricks. We must discover their mazes and movement.

La Cabane et le labyrinthe, Henri Gaudin

Hideaways are ingenious buildings that call on innovative solutions. Abbot Laugier saw primitive huts as precursors of the elegant neoclassical designs of his own day. Henri Gaudin, on the other hand, prefers the image of the medieval huts that sprang up on the flanks of fortresses and defensive walls. He writes, "A vision of urban architecture should be a vision of hideaways, parasitic structures such as stalls, huts, and other types of ephemeral architecture." The Archilab 2001 exhibition, held in Orléans, showed the vital role of such small constructions in the urban fabric, filling in the gaps in the saturated visual landscape. The architect Santiago Cirugeda Parejo planned an exhibit called "The mutant [and silent] architecture," which showed urban refuges where city dwellers could reclaim the space around them. For example, he transformed scaffolding and dumpsters on building sites into what he called "inhabitable prostheses." The problem of urban density has been particularly acute in Japan since the 1970s, and solutions such as "capsule hotels" have become part of the city landscape. Clients at these hotels sleep in miniature rooms barely larger than coffins, piled up like rows of safety deposit boxes in a bank.

"We must hark back to the beginnings, to huts, and to the fundamental, primitive question—what provides the best shelter? What hideaways are best suited to our post-industrial society?" The couple behind the Archimédia agency, Fiona Meadows and Frédéric Nantois, started out with the idea of a hideaway for one of their most ambitious projects, the Divorce House. They wanted to develop a new, playful, adaptable style of architecture, drawing on the mythology of the primitive huts described by Vitruvius. They were commissioned to design a vacation home for a couple in Normandy. As Fiona Meadows explains, "They wanted to start over, as they hated their home. We suggested that they move." Their new home was to represent a light-hearted new beginning. "If you just agree to forget your points of reference, your culture, and your values, you can totally reinvent the place you live in," explain Fiona and her partner Frédéric. "We decided to play on the hideaway's inherent instability and create an architectural style that did not just stick to tried and tested formulas, but invented its own language."

The Divorce House is very long and narrow—about nine feet wide and ninety feet long (three meters by thirty meters). It looks more like a garden shed than a traditional house. Fiona and Frédéric explain, "It is as wide as a corridor in a normal house. When you go through it from one end to the other, it's like going for a long walk. The rooms are decorated to create different atmospheres, and there are interior gardens, like a nature trail."

The Divorce House (facing page), designed by the architects Frédéric Nantois and Fiona Meadows, and set in the Normandy countryside, makes ironic reference to the materials used in garden sheds. The walls open up to reveal covered terraces, and part of the house, built in plastic, is on rails so that it can be pushed a few feet away from the main body of the building, in wood. The Sea, Sex, and Sun House (left) by the same architects was built in Benifallet in Catalonia (Spain), using reclaimed pallets and orange crates.

These fabulous lifeguards' cabins on Miami Beach (facing page) are like brightly colored candy scattered in the sand. Gilles Ebersolt's "wheeled bedroom" (right) takes its inspiration from wheelbarrows, and can be rolled on land or floated on a pond.

The Divorce House is anything but bland. In parts, the floor is planted with Astroturf, and the windows set in the walls of wood come from a mobile home. The main body of the building is divided into two parts, one in wood, the other in plastic. The walls can be folded back, so that the rooms open onto the covered terraces. "When the walls are folded back, the house loses its protective casing, and the border between inside and outside vanishes." The building techniques used were deliberately kept as low-tech as possible. The base is a concrete slab, the frame is of wood, and the rest of the house was simply put together like a jigsaw puzzle around the frame. The architects point out, "We made the building technique as simple as possible, like in a log cabin, so that practically all the tools we needed were a hammer and nails." The most extraordinary feature of the house is that part was built on rails. If either of the owners feels the need for privacy, they can slide part of the house eighty feet (twenty-five meters) along the rails.

The architects chose to entitle their revolutionary design the Divorce House because it represents a break with customary conceptions of the home and with architectural tradition, turning familiar notions of what makes a comfortable living space on their head. The narrow rooms would normally be judged impractical, but the owners love their fold-back walls and views over the Normandy countryside. The design also rejects the idea of the home as an investment. Like an ephemeral hideaway, the Divorce House was not planned as a nest-egg.

Many sociologists believe that in the twenty-first century, our society will become increasingly nomadic, thanks to mobile phones, laptop computers, and instant internet connections. Hideaways may well become emblematic of this new society, as they correspond to the key concepts of escapism and cocooning. Architects are increasingly catching on to the endless possibilities offered by their mobility—easy to put up, equally easy to pack away and rebuild elsewhere—and the way they fit into the gaps left in the urban landscape by more traditional architecture. In October 2002, the Tuileries Gardens in Paris showcased a number of up-and-coming young designers working on the theme of alternative architectural solutions. Gilles Ebersolt's nomadic constructions were among the most inventive. They included Ikos, a "cage for ornithologists," which was designed to be lifted by miniature airship to the rainforest canopy where it would hang from the branches, allowing the scientists to study birds and insects in their natural habitat. Ikos is a super-light structure built on an aluminum frame, containing a bed that doubles as a sofa, a table, and even a kitchen area. It can comfortably house three people for several days at a time. Another of Gilles Ebersolt's designs is the Ballule, a transparent bubble twelve feet (four meters) across, containing a cabin with room for one person. The Ballule was designed to roll down mountains and rivers.

The architects Claire Pétetin and Philippe Grégoire took the idea of a nomadic house to its conclusion in a design for a suitcase house. The design has not yet been developed beyond a blueprint, but the idea is intriguing: to meet the inhabitant's requirements in terms of space by a house that could be expanded and folded away like an accordion.

Designer hideaways

Designers Erwan and Ronan Bouroullec believe that we all need things which touch our emotions and our subconscious selves. Hideaways are one of these things. The Bouroullec brothers designed a hideaway presented at the Villa Noailles, in the town of Hyères on the French Riviera (above). It reflects their interest in micro-constructions. Facing page: the aluminum, steel, and lacquered wood "closed bed."

Box beds, sofas that double as indoor fortresses, carpets that can be turned into a magical tent. Indoor hideaways are hybrids, the missing link between furniture and buildings. Many ambitious young designers have found indoor hideaways to be a fruitful source of inspiration. Moving indoors from the garden, interior hideaways become a way for people to sidestep the issue of living between unyieldingly solid walls and to adapt the space of their apartment to their own needs.

The novelist Françoise Chandernagor recounts in her fictitious story of the life of Madame de Maintenon, the secret wife of the seventeenth-century king of France, Louis XIV how she described in letters a "niche" that she had built to protect her from the cold, and more particularly from prying eyes, in the royal palaces of Versailles, Fontainebleau, Marly, and Rambouillet. "The tyrant tolerated the 'niche' I invented to survive. It is a sort of large wardrobe without a door or floor, just walls and a ceiling. It is lined with padding and damask, with thick curtains half-hiding the front. Inside there is room for a sofa, an armchair, and a small table . . . to shelter from the frost and wind that prevail in this bedchamber."

Today, four centuries later, Madame de Maintenon would have a wealth of designs to choose from. There is Monica Foster's Cloud, a translucent plastic bubble that can be inflated and deflated in a matter of seconds. The fragile skin of the bubble is a protection against the stresses of the outside world. Matali Crasset has produced a number of designs on the theme of hideaways, including a carpet that doubles as a tent and her "Building Permit" sofa made of foam blocks that can be used to build an indoor fortress.

"Today, people need to tame the architecture they live in. They need to feel as if they have staked their claim on their space by putting up a tent!" The brothers Erwan and Ronan Bouroullec have long sought inspiration for their innovative designs in the imagery of the hideaway. "We predict a development of structures that will redefine apartments as a series of sheltering spaces. 1960s apartments were designed for families with two or three children. Today, this traditional image of the family unit is no longer valid. Lots of people live alone during the week and with three or four other people at the weekend." Their vision of micro-architecture is to make light, adaptable structures that people can put up and take down in minutes to transform their private space as required, creating intimate corners or on the contrary opening up wide spaces. By raising the floorboards or changing the lighting, they can totally alter the mood of an apartment, creating an illusion of escapism— after all, as the saying goes, a change is as good as a rest.

The Bouroullec brothers have also designed a contemporary spin on the traditional box bed, in metal and lacquered wood, mounted on piles between two and a half feet and nearly six feet (seventy to one hundred and eighty cm) tall. The box bed is designed to give a little privacy to couples without a bedroom of their own. The aluminum slats that form the walls of the box act like a screen of leaves. The wall looks solid from the outside, but people inside

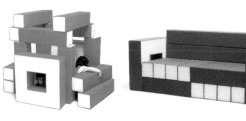

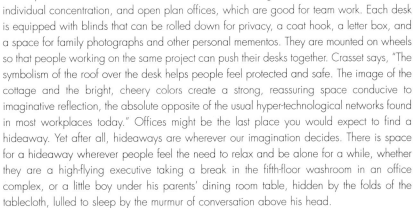

Matali Crasset, a former student of Philippe Starck, designed a village of office huts for the staff of the Red Cell advertising agency, based in Paris (facing page). She is strongly influenced by the colors and playful shapes of childhood, as seen in her "Building Permit" combination sofa and game for children (bottom right), which can be turned into a play fortress. The "function box" (top right) by Dante Donegani and Giovanni Lauda is ideal for relaxing and reading.

the box can peep out unseen. The brothers say, "Height is essential. Climbing on a stool or up a ladder to get into bed is a magnificent, symbolic action, like a rite signifying the passage from a shared to a private space. The symbolism of the hideaway is really all about this passage from a public space to a private, intimate world. It is wonderful to be able to go to ground for a while if you feel the need."

There is something infinitely reassuring about being in a hideaway. As we have seen, artists and writers go there to think and set their creativity flowing. The Museum of Modern Art in New York took this thought one step further in an exhibition entitled Workspheres. The designers and architects who participated were invited to consider the potential of workplaces on a human scale which encouraged true intellectual focus. They came up with modern versions of Victorian reading rooms or contemporary takes on the large oven where René Descartes is said to have elaborated his famous methodology of unified science.

Matali Crasset, a former student of Philippe Starck, took this idea even further in designing an office village for a Paris advertising agency. It is a fabulous place to work—the advertising executives work on desks shaped like little cottages, and the walls are painted in bright lemon yellow and azure blue. These office hideaways are a compromise between individual offices, which are good for individual concentration, and open plan offices, which are good for team work. Each desk is equipped with blinds that can be rolled down for privacy, a coat hook, a letter box, and a space for family photographs and other personal mementos. They are mounted on wheels so that people working on the same project can push their desks together. Crasset says, "The symbolism of the roof over the desk helps people feel protected and safe. The image of the cottage and the bright, cheery colors create a strong, reassuring space conducive to imaginative reflection, the absolute opposite of the usual hyper-technological networks found in most workplaces today." Offices might be the last place you would expect to find a hideaway. Yet after all, hideaways are wherever our imagination decides. There is space for a hideaway wherever people feel the need to relax and be alone for a while, whether they are a high-flying executive taking a break in the fifth-floor washroom in an office complex, or a little boy under his parents' dining room table, hidden by the folds of the tablecloth, lulled to sleep by the murmur of conversation above his head.

In the present rethinking of why we build and what we build for, the primitive hut will, I suggest, retain its validity as a reminder of the original and therefore essential meaning of all building for people: that is, of architecture.... I believe, therefore, that it will continue to offer a pattern to anyone concerned with building, a primitive hut situated permanently perhaps beyond the reach of the historian or archeologist, in some place I must call Paradise. And paradise is a promise as well as a memory.

On Adam's House in Paradise, Joseph Rykwert

BUYER'S GUIDE

For me, the hut is a crude, light construction, whose only builder was its inhabitant. Of course, I am thinking of Robinson Crusoe.

Michel Tournier

The MontOZ'arbres treetop bedroom in the Pyrenees.

The definition given by Michel Tournier, author of the novel *Friday or the Other Island*, a reworking of the Robinson Crusoe story, is apt. A hideaway's character depends on a number of factors—the shape of the tree, the choice between the eagle's nest perched high in the branches or the warm lair huddled at the foot of the trunk. Then there is the choice of materials and styles—wood; sheet metal; a round yurt, the structure draped in brightly colored fabric; or a solid chalet made of pine logs. Then the building begins—sometimes immensely satisfying, as when the first wall is finished, and sometimes endlessly frustrating, as when the doors and windows stick and refuse to open. It is a long process, wearing on the nerves, and definitely not advised for the impatient by nature...

Not everybody is as inventive or resourceful as Robinson Crusoe. Fortunately, a number of companies now specialize in

A seashell hut designed by Marielle Mouterde.

building hideaways, helping you every step of the way, providing everything from the initial plans to the final furnishings. The artists, architects, landscape architects, and designers listed in this guide are always glad to help with advice, whatever your project—designing a hideaway from scratch, or buying a ready-made garden shed to personalize with grandfather's armchair and grandmother's velvet cushions, a few well-chosen books and souvenirs of vacations past.

This guide has all the information you need to plan the hideaway of your dreams, whether your secret wish is to get away from it all in a Gypsy caravan, vacation in a yurt, or sleep in the treetops and be woken by the birds.

Designers and Architects

Antoine Arnoux
His "Unicorn Garden" is full of hideaways and huts, one in trompe-l'oeil, one in an old London bus.
Les Jardins de la Licorne
La Croix-Buée
14130 Saint-André-d'Hebertot - France
Tel.: +33 (0)6 87 06 69 01
See photos pages 110–111.

Atelier Virginie Écorce
Cyril Delage and Virginie Écorce build garden shelters in chestnut wood. Their creations are absolutely unique, fitted snugly around the trunk of a tree or tucked in a corner of the garden.
Route départementale 901
87500 Le Chalard - France
Tel.: +33 (0)5 55 08 28 04
See pages 20, 21, 97.

Hugues Peuvergne
The landscape architect Hugues Peuvergne specializes in garden hideaways. His designs can be adapted to any space, whether in the country or the heart of the city.
42, bis avenue du Général-Leclerc
77400 Lagny-sur-Marne - France
Tel.: +33 (0)1 64 30 61 75
See pages 46, 82, 90, 92, 106.

L'île Instant
The artist Mathieu Ducournau and the architect Philippe Le Moal design pine sheds in the shape of barges, wheelbarrows, and benches. They are delivered in flat packs so that the owners can feel pride in having built their own shed.
1, rue Ernest-Le-Barzic
22450 La Roche-Derrien - France

Tel.: +33 (0)6 12 53 30 73
or (0)6 68 51 30 34
See pages 50, 51.

Tree House Workshop
Peter Nelson and Jake Jacob design
and build made-to-measure tree houses,
and help clients who wish to plan
and build to their own design.
Tree House Workshop, Inc.
303 N.W. 43rd - Seattle
WA 98107 - U.S.
Tel.: +1 (206) 784-2112
Fax.: +1 (206) 784-1424
Email: anna@treehouseworkshop.com
www.treehouseworkshop.com
See photo page 140.

François Rochoux
One of the last remaining masters of rocaille
work. He designs and builds rocaille pieces
on commission.
125, rue Caulaincourt
75018 Paris - France
Tel.: +33 (0)1 42 23 72 16
See photo page 99.

La cabane perchée
Alain Laurens and Daniel Dufour design
and build luxury tree houses in red cedar
wood, without using nails that could damage
the tree trunk. They even offer models with
built-in lightning conductors and solar panels.
La campagne Bertet
84480 Bonnieux - France
Tel.: +33 (0)4 90 75 91 40
www.la-cabane-perchee.com
See photos pages 8, 9, 35, 36, 37.

Marielle Mouterde
A passionate collector of seashells, Marielle
Mouterde builds children's hideaways

A cottage by the Belgian designers Kabane.

which she decorates with pebbles,
fragments of blue glass, and shells.
555, rue Albert-Bailly
59700 Marcq-en-Baroeul - France
Tel.: +33 (0)3 20 36 78 27
Photo facing page.

La Vannerie d'hier, aujourd'hui
Éric Renault is a craftsman working in wicker,
using live willow and dried wicker to make
gazebos or bowers. His creations are playful,
exploiting various techniques and emotions.
5, rue du Lieu-dit La Barrurie-Saunay
37110 Château-Renault - France
Tel.: +33 (0)2 47 56 93 09
See pages 30, 103.

Philippe Stoffaes
A landscape architect with a passion for
hideaways.

La Maïlonerie
24420 Sorges - France
Tel.: +33 (0)5 53 46 70 37
See page 99 (top left).

Joël Rouillé
Weaves wicker hideaways, domes, teepees,
pergolas, and igloos.
7, rue de Masselière
37190 Vilaines-les-Rochers - France
Tel.: +33 (0)2 47 45 33 14
www.joel-rouille-osier.com

TreeHouse Company
The famous Scottish company founded
by John Harris designs and builds
superb tree houses for children
and families, and can even give
their designs an authentically weathered
look on request.

A playhouse on stilts by the Belgian designers Kabane.

The Stables
Maunsheugh Road
Fenwick, Ayrshire
KA3 6AN - Scotland, U.K.
Tel.: +44 (0)1560 600111
www.treehouse-company.com
See pages 22, 25, 32, 40, 41.

Living Tree, LLC
Based in the United States, Jonathan Fairoaks is an ISA Certified Arborist with over forty years of experience in building tree houses.
Tel.: +1 (610) 952-5209
or (530) 320-6444
Email: treehouse@livingtreeonline.com
www.livingtreeonline.com

Skillful Means
An architectural and construction firm active in sustainable resources and straw-bale design that is also available for talks, workshops and on-site guidance.
P.O. Box 207
Junction City
CA 96048 - U.S.
Tel..: +1 (530) 623-4479
Fax.: +1 (530) 623-5579
Email: contact@skillful-means.com
www.skillful-means.com

Kabane
The Belgian designers Virginie and Marco Sneiders build wooden hideaways in all styles, from simple huts to sophisticated designs on stilts. They offer a range of ready-made designs and also work to order.
8, rue de l'Église-Saint-Étienne
1380 Ohain - Belgium
Tel.: +32 26 33 68 26
See pages 54, 134.

François Houtin
An engraver and draftsman who also designs and builds hideaways.
15, rue Madame
75006 Paris - France
Tel.: +33 (0)1 45 44 21 70
Email: fhoutin@art11.com
See pages 33, 94, 99, 100, 101, 102.

Build your own hideaway kits

Wood for good
This British trade association sells wooden huts for children and adults alike, for use as tree houses or on the ground. For each tree cut down, the association ensures that two are planted.
33 Rosebery Road
London
N10 2LE - England, U.K.
Tel.: +44 (0)20 8365 2700
www.woodforgood.com

Lawsons
1208 High Rd.
London
N20 OLL - England, U.K.
Tel.: +44 (0)20 8446 7321
www.lawsons.co.uk

Shelter Kit Incorporated
Barn and loft-style houses.
22 W Mill Street
Tilton
NH 03276 - U.S.
Tel.: +1 (603) 286-7611
Fax: +1 (603) 286-2839
Email: buildings@shelterkit.com

Two playhouses by Cottage Company.

Backyard America
Discount residential outdoor structures
available to order online.
7606 Centreville Road
Manassas
VA 20111 - U.S.
Tel.: +1 (703) 392-5152
Toll Free: (877) 489-8064
Fax: +1 (703) 257-5346
www.backyardamerica.com

Summerwood Products
A wide array of products, including
cabins, studios, playhouses and garden
sheds in kit format.
735 Progress Ave.
Toronto
ON M1H 2W7 - Canada
Email: info@summerwood.com
www.summerwood.com

Spirit Elements
Ready-to-assemble cabins, cabanas,
and children's playhouses.
1495 Yarmouth Avenue
Boulder
CO 80304 - U.S.
Tel.: +1 (303) 998-1440
Email: cs@spiritelements.com
www.spiritelements.com

Gardensheds
651 Millcross Rd.
Lancaster
PA 17601 - U.S.
Tel.: +1 (717) 397-5430
www.gardensheds.com

HomePlace Structures
A family business that produces hand-crafted
wood products, including Log Cabin kits,
gazebos, and children's playhouses
by Amish craftsmen.
176 South New Holland Rd.
Gordonville
PA 17529 - U.S.
Tel.: +1 (866) 768-8465
www.homeplacestructures.com

Exhibitions

Rêves de cabanes
Every summer, the nurseryman Philippe Burey
opens his gardens to hideaways of all shapes
and sizes.
Les jardins de la Brande
D21
24380 Fouleix - France
Tel.: +33 (0)5 53 07 47 85
See pages 20–21 and 95.

The company Les Roulottiers make caravans of all kinds, from the kinds seen in Westerns to romantic Gypsy styles.

The Chaumont-sur-Loire Garden Festival

Held annually. Every year, the festival has a given theme that the thirty featured gardeners are invited to interpret as they wish.
www.chaumont-jardins.com
See pages 86, 87, 106.

Exploring the treetops

MontOZ'arbres

Leads expeditions through the treetops, with an overnight stay in a tree house.
La Gallinée Route d'Espagne
66230 Prats de Mollo la Preste
France
Tel.: +33 (0)4 68 39 72 76
www.montozarbres.com
See pages 39, 131.

Do-it-yourself Courses

Out 'n' About Treesort and Treehouse Institute

Host of the World Treehouse Association's annual convention every October on Columbus Day weekend, the Treesort and Treehouse Institute offers courses in tree-house construction, as well as outdoor activities such as rafting expeditions and horseback riding.
300 Page Crk. Rd.
Cave Jct.
OR 97523 - U.S.
Tel.: +1 (541) 592-2208
Email: treesort@treehouses.com
www.treehouses.com

Caravans

Les Roulottiers

Laurent Reynaud and Christelle Bataille build caravans in Arles, in the south of France.

ZI Sud Quai Jean-Charcot
13200 Arles - France
Tel.: +33 (0)4 90 18 58 29
& (0)6 61 81 58 95
Fax: +33 (0)4 90 93 58 40
Email: contact@lesroulottiers.com
www.lesroulottiers.com
See photograph left.

Jeanne Bayol

Renovates antique gypsy and fairground caravans.
Mas des Verdines
13000 Saint-Rémy-de-Provence - France
Tel.: +33 (0)4 32 60 03 26

Staying in a caravan

In recent years, more and more hotels have begun offering overnight stays in caravans.

Hôtel Mas dou Pastre

route Orgon
13810 Eygalières - France
Tel.: +33 (0)4 90 95 92 61
See page 75.

Mayo Horse Drawn Caravan Holidays

Belcarra
Castlebar
County Mayo - Ireland
Tel.: +353 943 2054
Email: post@mayoholidays.com

Into the West 2000 Horse Drawn Caravans

Cartron House Farm
Ballinakill
Kylebrack
Loughrea
County Galway - Ireland

Tel.: +353 5094 5211
Email: cartronhouse@hotmail.com

Kilvahan Horse Drawn Caravans
Kilvahan
Portlaoise
County Laois - Ireland
Tel.: +353 5022 7048
Email: kilvahan@eircom.net

Slattery's Horse Drawn Caravans
1 Russell Street
Tralee
County Kerry - Ireland
Tel.: +353 66718 6240
Email: caravanes@slatterys.com

Gerdien Bronkhorst
Landmetersveld 910
7327 KG Apeldoorn
The Netherlands
tel.: +31 55 540 14 47
fax: +31 55 540 14 48
Email: ge.bronkhorst@chello.nl

Yurts

Pacific Yurts Inc.
Designer and manufacturer of modern yurts.
77456 Hwy 99 South
Cottage Grove
OR 97424 - U.S.
Tel.: +1 (541) 942-9435
Email: info@yurts.com
www.yurts.com

Oregon Yurtworks, Inc.
Specializing in prefabricated
modular yurts.
1285 Wallis Street
Eugene
OR 97402 - U.S.

A yurt made in Brittany by Atelier des Trois Yourtes.

Tel.: +1 (541) 343-5330
Email: info@yurtworks.com
www.yurtworks.com

Hal Wynne-Jones
Hal Wynne-Jones fell in love with
traditional Mongolian yurts on
a visit to Central Asia. Since then,
he has set up his own company
making yurts.
Hullasey Barn, Tarlton
Cirencester, Gloucestershire
England, U.K.
Tel./fax: +44 (0)1285 770 773
Email: Halwj@hotmail.com

Charles Leys: Atelier des Trois Yourtes
Offers courses in building a yurt,
based in Brittany.
6, rue des Vergers
35330 Les Brulais - France
Tel.: +33 (0)2 99 92 47 82

www.yourtes.fr
See page 76 and above.

Vacationing in a hideaway

Les sources de Caudalie
This luxurious spa now offers guests an
overnight stay in an offshore hideaway after
a day enjoying their vinotherapy beauty
treatments.
Chemin de Smith-Haut-Lafitte
33650 Bordeaux-Martillac - France
www.sources-caudalie.com
Tel.: +33 (0)5 57 83 83 83
Fax: +33 (0)5 57 83 83 84
See pages 56–57.

Cedar Creek Treehouse
A mountain retreat fifty feet up in a giant
cedar tree of the lush temperate rainforest with
a view of Mount Rainier from your bedroom.

P.O. Box 204
Ashford
WA 98304 - U.S.
Tel.: +1 (360) 569-2991
Email: treehouse@marshell.com

Lothlorien Woods Hide-A-Way
Tree-house keeper Jeal Breckenridge has
created her own one-of-a-kind tree-house
fantasy, in the deep woods of Gifford Pinchot
National Forest, which she has been sharing
with guests since 2001.
P.O. Box 1697
White Salmon
WA 98672 - U.S.
Tel.: +1 (509) 493-TREE

Treehouses of Hawaii
Three tree houses with ocean views
that are part of a twenty-acre flower farm
on the east side of Maui.
www.treehousesofhawaii.com

Post Ranch Inn
Nestled within ninety-eight acres of a fragile
ecosystem, individual luxury tree-house
accommodations are built nine feet off the
ground, on stilts, with a stairway to each
entrance. Triangular in shape, each room has
a bed in the center with a window seat, desk,
and fireplace in the corner. Glorious views
shine through windows on all sides.
Highway 1
P.O. Box 219
Big Sur
CA 93920 - U.S.
Tel.: +1 (831) 667-2200
Fax: +1 (831) 667-2824
Email: info@postranchinn.com

Treehouse Cottages
Three luxury tree-house cottages complete with
suspension walking bridge access.

165 W Van Buren
Eureka Springs
AR 72632 - U.S.
Tel.: +1 (479) 253-8667
Email: info@treehousecottages.com
www.treehousecottages.com

The Treehouse Camp, Maple Tree Campground
A basic tree-house campground that offers
a truly rustic, no-frills camping experience.
20716 Townsend Road
Gapland
Maryland 21779 - U.S.
Tel.: +1 (301) 432-5585
Email: treehousecamp2@aol.com
www.treehousecamp.com

Niassam Hills Lodge
On the road to Palmarin, some ninety-five
miles (one hundred and sixty km) from Dakar,
the lodge lies between a lagoon and the
savanna. It was built using all natural
materials. Book one of the rooms in the
branches of the giant baobabs.
Palmarin Ngallou, Pointe de Djiffer
Siné-Saloum - Senegal
Tel.: (00.221) 669 63 43
www.niassam.com
See page 77.

Matusadona Lodge
Wilderness Safaris
P.O. Box 288, Victoria Falls
Zimbabwe
Tel.: 263 134 527
Email: rita@wilderness.co.zu
See page 78.

Swedish design
There are more than three hundred cottages
and cabins for rent in the travel brochure
Destination Stockholm Archipelago.

Contact the Swedish Tourist Office
or the site www.dess.se for further details.

Utter Inn (Otter Inn)
Designed by Svensk Samtidskonst,
this little red-and-white-painted cabin
is floating in the middle of a lake.
The underwater bedrooms have
panoramic windows with views
of the depths of the lake and the fish.
Tomtebogatan 26
113 38 Stockholm - Sweden
Tel.: (+46) 70 775 5 393
Contact Mikael Genderg: 021-830023;
mikael@konst.org
www.konst.org/genberg
See page 50.

La Maison du voyageur
This company in Kyrgystan offers
vacations in yurts.
La Maison du Voyageur
122 Moskovskai
72 00 00 Bichkek - Kyrgystan
Tel.: (+996) 312 66 63 30
Email: kyrgyzdos@mail.kg
or kyrgyzdos@elcat.kg

Designer Hideaways

The Red Cube
The Red Cube was designed in 1997
by the artist Gloria Friemann and
the architect Adelfo Scaranello as
a "hideaway artwork." It stands on
the shores of a lake in the heart of
the French countryside. It was designed
to put visitors in touch with nature:
there is no running water or electricity,
and the interior decoration is deliberately
plain—just bricks and wood.
One wall of the cube is all in glass.

It can be booked by parties of up
to six for a weekend or a week.
Bookings: Solange Guenin
Route de Santenoge
52160 Villars-Santenoge - France
Tel.: +33 (0)3 25 84 22 10
Fax: +33 (0)3 80 30 59 74
See pages 112, 120.

Matali Crasset

The designer's tent-carpet and
"Building Permit" sofa of soft
sponge bricks are available from
Domeau and Pérès.
Tel.: +33 (0)1 47 60 93 86
www.domeau-peres.com
See pages 128–129.

Erwan and Ronan Bouroullec

The cupboard-bed designed
by the two brothers is available
from Cappellini.
4, rue des Rosiers
75004 Paris - France.
Their indoor parasol and
foam hideaways are available
from Kreo.
22, rue Duchefdelaville
75013 Paris - France
Tel.: +33 (0)1 53 60 18 42
www.kreo.co
See pages 126–127.

Gilles Ebersolt

Trained as an engineer, the architect
Gilles Ebersolt now designs
ultra-modern inflatable tree houses
and hideaways.
Agence d'architecture
60, rue Truffaut
75017 Paris - France
Tel.: +33 (0)1 42 29 39 74
See page 125.

An allotment shed in Amiens, in the Picardy region of northern France.

Hideaways to visit

Ferme de Gally
La Ferme de Gally, a petting zoo outside
Paris, has several unusual hideaways,
including a tree house, one shaped like
a wheelbarrow.
Ferme de Gally
Route de Bailly
78210 Saint-Cyr-l'Ecole - France
Tel.: +33 (0)1 30 14 60 60
See photo page 142.

Les hortillonnages d'Amiens
Hire a boat from the Auberge
de la Mère Boule on the towpath
and explore the canals that weave
in and out of the allotments
on each bank.
54 bd de Beauvillé
80000 Amiens - France
Tel.: +33 (0)3 22 91 31 66
See page 139.

*A Canadian tree house, designed by Peter and
Judy Nelson from the company Treehouse
Workshop.*

Bibliography

General works:
• Boyer, Marie-France. *Cabin Fever*. New
York: Thames and Hudson, 1995.
• Burey, Philippe. *Rêves de cabanes*. Éditions
les jardins de la Brande, 2002.
• *Cabanes, cabanons et campements*.
Travaux de la Société d'Écologie Humaine.
Bordeaux: Éditions de Bergier, 1999.
• Denbury, Jo. *Heavens and Hideaways*.
London; New York: Ryland Peters and Small,
2002.
• Nelson, Peter and Judy, with David Larkin.
The Treehouse Book. New York: Universe
Publications, 2000.
• Pearson, David. *Treehouses*. The House
that Jack Built, Gaia Books, 2001.
• Thorburn, Gordon. *Men and Sheds*. New
Holland Publishers, 2002.
• Tixier, Jean Max. *Le cabanon*. Marseille:
Éditions Jeanne Laffitte.

Articles:
• Faure, Sonya. "La hutte finale," in
"Tentations," *Libération* (September 14, 2001).
• Kerchouche, Dalila. "L'appel de la forêt,"
L'Express (April 26, 2001).
• Lis, Céline. "Ma cabane les pieds dans
l'eau," *L'Express* (August 17, 2000).
• "Micro-architectures," in *L'architecture
d'aujourd'hui*, CCCXXXVIII. Paris: June 2000.
• Millot, Ondine. "Mon sacre à la
tronçonneuse," in "Tentations," *Libération*
(May 31, 2002).

Literary Hideaways:
• Bachelard, Gaston. *Poetics of Space*.
New York: Orion Press, 1964.
• Cadiot, Olivier. *Retour définitif et durable
de l'être aimé*. Paris: P.O.L.
• Calvino, Italo. *The Baron in the Trees*.
New York: Random House, 1959.

• Cocteau, Jean. *Les Enfants Terribles*.
New York: Brewer & Warren Inc., 1930.
• Defoe, Daniel. *Robinson Crusoe*.
New York: Chelsea House, 1995.
• Sanchez, Catherine, ed. *En cabanes*.
Opales, 1998.
• Gide, André, tr. Dorothy Bussy. *Fruits of the
Earth*. New York: Alfred A. Knopf, 1949.
• Goethe, Johann Wolfgang von, tr. David
Constantine. *Elective Affinities*. Oxford;
New York: Oxford University Press, 1994.
• Izzo, Jean-Claude. *Total Khéops, Solea et
Chourmo: la trilogie marseillaise*. Paris: Gallimard.
• Kamo No Chomei. *An Account of My Hut*.
Pawlet, VT.: Banyan Press, 1976.
• Kamo No Onomei. *The Ten Foot Square
Hut*. Sydney: Robertson, 1928.
• Le Clezio, Jean-Marie. *Pawana*. Paris:
Gallimard, 2003.
• Le Drian, Marie. *La Cabane d'Hippolyte*.
Paris: Julliard, 2001.
• Lawrence, David Herbert. *Lady Chatterley's
Lover*. Cambridge; New York: Cambridge
University Press, 1993.
• Rousseau, Jean-Jacques. *Discourse on the
origin of inequality*. Indianapolis: Hackett
Pub. Co., 1992.
• Salinger, Margaret. *Dream Catcher*.
New York: Washington Square Press, 2000.
• Thoreau, Henry David. *Walden*. London:
Dent/Everyman's Library, 1968.
• Verne, Jules. *The Mysterious Island*. New
York: Scribner's, 1988.
• Weber, Marie-Helène. *Robinson et
Robinsonnades: étude comparée de Robinson
Crusoë de Defoe, Le Robinson suisse de J.-R.
Wyss, L'Île mystérieuse de Jules Verne, Sa
majesté des mouches de W. Golding,
Vendredi ou les limbes du Pacifique de M.
Tournier*, Ed. Universitaires du Sud, 1993.

Childhood Hideaways:
• Anzieu, Didier. *L'Enfant et sa maison*. Paris:
Centre de guidance infantile, E.S.F., 1988.

A hideaway at the Ferme de Gally petting zoo in Saint-Cyr-l'École, near Paris.

• Bettelheim, Bruno. *The Uses of Enchantment: The Meaning and Importance of Fairy Tales.* New York: Vintage Books, 1977.
• Bosco, Henri. *L'Enfant et la rivière.* Paris: Gallimard, 1977.
• Bru, Josiane, "L'Arbre-cabane et autres refuges dans les contes populaires," in *Micro-architectures, L'architecture d'aujourd'hui,* CCCXXVIII (June 2000). Éditions Jean-Michel Place.
• Grimm, Jacob. *Fairy Tales.* New York: Knopf: Distributed by Random House, 1992.

• *Il était une fois ... les contes de fées,* catalogue of exhibition "Il était une fois ... les contes de fées." Paris: Bibliothèque Nationale de France, 2001.
• Pergaud, Louis. *La guerre des boutons.* Paris: Folio, 2001.
• Ségur, Countess of. *The Vacation.* Paris: Folio Junior, 1982.
• Tournier, Michel. *Friday and Robinson.* New York: Knopf, 1972.
• Twain, Mark. *The Adventures of Huckleberry Finn.* New York: Norton, 1977.

• Twain, Mark. *The Adventures of Tom Sawyer.* Boston; New York: Ginn and Company, 1931.

Yurts and Caravans:
• Bayol, Jeanne. *Rêves de roulettes.* Aix-en-Provence: Edisud, 2000.
• Delpont, Léa; Lis, Céline. "Nomades chics: choisissez votre camp," *L'Express* (May 30, 2002).
• Duboy, Philippe. "L'esprit nouveau: la villa nomade de Raymond Roussel," in *Micro-architectures, L'architecture d'aujourd'hui,* CCCXXVIII (June 2000).
• Miyuki Aoki. "Habitat nomade d'Anatolie: une architecture auto-porteuse," in *Micro-architectures, L'architecture d'aujourd'hui,* CCCXXVIII (June 2000).
• Pearson, David. *Freewheeling homes.* The House that Jack Built, Gaia Books, 2002.
• Pearson, David. *Yurts, tipis and Benders.* The House that Jack Built, Gaia Books, 2001.
• "Profile: Hal Wynne-Jones, yurt makers," *Gardens Illustrated* (July/August, 2001).

Garden Sheds:
• Brun, Bernard. "La cabane et l'écologie humaine," in *Cabanes, cabanons et campements, Travaux de la société d'écologie humaine.* Bordeaux: Éditions de Bergier, 1999.
• Cavanna, François; Meaille, Patricia. *Au fond du jardin.* Rennes: Terre de brume, 2002.
• Jones, Louisa. *Nouveaux jardins de campagne.* Paris: Albin Michel, 2000.
• Pigeat, Jean-Louis. *Les Paysages de la vigne.* Paris: Solar, 2000.
• Tiberghien, Gilles A. *Nature, art, paysage.* Arles: Actes Sud, 2001.

Gardens

• Bouquin, Edith Claude. "Les abris de jardins," in *Cent ans d'histoire des Jardins ouvriers, 1896-1996: la Ligue française du coin de terre et du foyer*, edited by Béatrice Cabedoce and Philippe Pierson. Grane: Créaphis, 1996.

• Hissart, Jean-René; Portet, François. "Les jardins ouvriers de Belfort," in *Traverses*, V-VI (June1976), pp. 171–191.

• Dubost, Françoise. "Le cabanon du dimanche," in *Les premiers Banlieusards*. Grane: Créaphis.

• Virieu, Claire de; Laroze, Catherine. *Un jardin pour soi*. Arles: Acte Sud, 1996.

• Weber, Florence. *L'honneur des jardiniers: les potagers dans la France du xxe siècle*. Paris: Éditions Belin, 1998.

Follies:

• Bénétière, Marie-Hélène. *Jardin: vocabulaire typologique et technique*, edited by Monique Chatenet and Monique Mosser. Paris: Centre des monuments nationaux, Éditions du Patrimoine, 2000.

• Claisse, Jules. *Le Plessis-Robinson: de d'Artagnan aux dimanches de Robinson, des cités-jardins au Hiboux d'aujourd'hui*. Le Plessis-Robinson: Éditions La Ville, 1984.

• Fontaine, Marie-Madeleine. "Mécènes aux jardins," in *Jardin notre double: sagesse and déraison*, edited by Hervé Brunon. Paris: Autrement, 1999.

• Plumptre, Georges. *L'ornement de jardin*. Thames and Hudson.

• Richardson, Phyllis. *Big Ideas: Small Buildings*. New York: Universe Publishing, 2001.

• Saudan, Michel; Saudon-Skyra, Sylvia. *From Folly to Follies: Discovering the World of Gardens*. New York: Abbeville Press, 1988.

Architectural Hideaways:

• Catalogue Archilab, Orléans, 2001.

• Chimbreto, Bruno. *Le Corbusier à Cap Martin*. Marseille: Éditions Parenthèses, 1987.

• Gaudin, Henri. *La cabane et le labyrinthe*. Sprimont (Belgium): Éditions Mardaga; Collection Architecture et Recherches.

• Loubes, Jean Paul. "La cabane, figure poétique de l'architecture," in *Cabanes, cabanons et campements, Travaux de la société d'écologie humaine*. Bordeaux: Éditions de Bergier, 1999.

• Papillault, Rémi. "Le Corbusier, le bon sauvage en son cabanon," in *Micro-architectures, L'architecture d'aujourd'hui*, CCCXXVIII (June 2000).

• Richardson, Phyllis, *Big Ideas: Small Buildings*. New York: Universe Publishing, 2001.

• Rykwert, Joseph. *On Adam's House in Paradise; the idea of the primitive hut in architectural history*. New York: Museum of Modern Art; distributed by New York Graphic Society, Greenwich, Conn., 1972.

• Sowa, Axel. "Les hôtels-capsules au Japon," in *Micro-architectures, L'architecture d'aujourd'hui*, CCCXXVIII (June 2000).

• Vilder, Anthony. *L'espace des Lumières: architecture and philosophie de Ledoux à Fourier*. Paris: Édition Picard, 1995.

• Wines, James. *L'architecture Verte*, Taschen, 2002.

Websites:

• www.sitewan.org/cabanes
A very interesting site with numerous photographs and texts by architects and philosophers. In French.

• On the Copenhagen Architecture Garden: www.arcspace.com.

• The Chaumont-sur-Loire Garden Festival: www.chaumont-jardins.com

Photographic Credits

Guillaume de Laubier: 1, 6–7, 34, 36, 37, 59, 70, 121; Jérôme Darblay: 2–3, 10, 24, 45 (top), 52, 53, 54, 55, 64, 134; Patrick Von Robaeys: 4–5 (styling L. Lajouanie); Nicolas Bruant: 8, 9; Philippe Sarahoff: 11; George Amann: 12–13; Philippe Perdereau: 14, 21, 83, 84, 135 (right); Roger Viollet: 16, 28, 104, 105, 109; All rights reserved-Opération "Cabanes, construis ton aventure" p. 17, 18 (top left): "Cabanes éphémères" by the class of Marie-Dominique Rouquier, Robert Schumann School, Etréchy; p. 18 (top right): "La cabane au fond du jardin" by the class of Anne-Marie Jeault, Pierre and Marie Curie School, Cébazat; p. 18 (bottom): "La cabane folle" by the class of Anne-Christine Gimenez, Ilet School, Bourse Mafate, Possession; p. 19: "La cabane du quatrième petit cochon" by the class of Anne Rasse, Pajol-Torcy School, Paris; TreeHouse: 22, 25, 32, 40, 41; Marianne Majerus: 23, 93; Gérard Franquin, *Boucle d'or* (Flammarion): 26; Claude Ponti, *Okilélé* (L'école des loisirs): 29; Thomas Dupaigne: 30, 31, 87, 88, 90, 91, 92, 95, 97, 99 (bottom right), 100, 101, 106, 135 (left), 142; François Houtin: 33, 94, 99 (top right and bottom left), 102. Indian ink wash. By kind permission of the Galerie Michèle Broutta; Photo Clarisse: 20, 80, 82, 89, 96, 99 (top left).103, 110, 111; Wade/Bios: 38; Noël Hautemanière: 39, 130; Joël Laiter: 44, 45 (bottom); Solvi Dos Santos: 42, 43; Deidi von Schaeven: 46; Hugues Peuvergne: 47; Delphine Warin: 48, 51; François Rascalou/Bios: 49; Michaël Genberg: 50; Les Sources de Caudalie: 56–57; G B: 58; Christian Sarramon: 60, 65, 74, 75, 85, 118, 119; Cécil Mathieu: 61; Renaud Dengreville: 62; Juan Espi: 66; Alain Baudry: 67; Anna Garde: 68, 69; Frédéric Vasseur: 72, 73; Charles Leys: 76, 137; Hill Lodge: 77; Erick Saillet: 78; Alex Petzold: 86, 139; Victor Petit, extract from *Country habitations, including houses, villas, chalets, pavilions, kiosks, parks, and gardens* (1848): 107–108; André Morin: 112, 120; Edouard Böthlink: 114–115; Atelier van Lieshout B. V.: 116–117; ADAGP, 118,119; 2003 archi media – Fiona Meadows + Frédéric Nantois: 122–123; Serge Ollivier: 124; Gilles Ebersolt: 125; Erwan and Ronan Bouroullec: 126–127; Roberto Baldessari: 129 top; Patrick Gries: 128, 129 (bottom); Christine Ternynck: 132; Kabane: 133; Christelle Bataille: 136; Paul Rocheleau: 140.

Index

The companies featured in the buyer's guide are not listed in the index.

Acknowledgments

The author wishes to extend her warmest thanks to Anne-Marie Fèvre, who got her interested in huts and hideaways in the first place, Pierre Bernard, Valérie Picaudé, Delphine Dollfus, Inès Gaulès, and everyone at the Institut Français d'Architecture for the wealth of information they were able to provide on the children's architecture project "Construis ton aventure," Josiane Bru, Bernard Picon, and Laurence Nicolas for their unstinting help and the many hours spent discussing this book, Fabrice Barthélémy who read and re-read the many drafts, and all the people who share my interest for hideaways in all shapes and forms, and who often gave me ideas for this book. The editors wish to thank all the designers and architects who lent material for the project. Special thanks go to François Iselin and Flora Dumoulin for their precious help.

Editor: **Ghislaine Bavoillot**
Translated from the French by:
Susan Pickford
Copyediting: **Slade Smith**
Typesetting: **Thierry Renard**
Proofreading: **Linda Gardiner**
Color separation: **Penez Édition**

Previously published in French as *Cabanes*
© Éditions Flammarion, 2003
English-language edition
© Éditions Flammarion, 2004
26, rue Racine
75006 Paris
www.editions.flammarion.com

04 05 06 4 3 2 1

FC0451-04-III
ISBN: 2-0803-0451-8
Dépôt légal: 03/2004

Printed in France by Pollina - N° I92341